Nurturing the Souls of Our Children

D1564557

Nurturing the Souls of Our Children

What Children Need and What Parents Can Do

Thomas F. Geary Bonnie L. Geary

SMYTH&HELWYS
PUBLISHING, INCORPORATED · MACON, GEORGIA
WWW.HELWYS.COM

To Kathleen and Michael

who taught us much about souls.

Acknowledgements

We are grateful to the following: Bonnie Milani, who guided our writing with professionalism and care; Michael Toth, who offered invaluable suggestions and showed much patience; Sally Taylor, Joan Barry McGuire, Kathleen Geary and Michael Geary for reading the manuscript; and Michael Murphy for his generous help.

Smyth & Helwys Publishing, Inc.
6316 Peake Road
Macon, Georgia 31210-3960
1-800-747-3016
©2002 by Smyth & Helwys Publishing

Library of Congress Cataloging-in-Publication Data

Geary, Thomas F.
    Nurturing the Souls of our children: what every child needs, what every
    parent can do / Thomas F. Geary, Bonnie L. Geary.
    p. cm.
    Originally published: Valencia, California: M.W. Murphy, 1999
    ISBN 1-57312-322-6 (pbk)
    1. Parenting—Religious aspects—Christianity.
    2. Parenting—Psychological aspects.
    I. Geary, Bonnie L. II.
    II. Title

    BV4526.3 .G43 2002
    248.8'45—dc21
                                                    2001055029
                                                         CIP

Table of Contents

Introduction

This book is about the soul of a child. It is a guide for parents (and anyone else who deals with children) to search for, touch, and nurture the soul of their child by staying psychologically and spiritually balanced. We are not speaking of soul only in a religious sense. We are not advocating any specific religious belief. We are talking about a deeper appreciation of an individual child. Who is she? Who is he? Apart from norms? Apart from others? Apart from his academic scores or other measurements? What are his dreams? What are his struggles? What are her fears? What does she feel about her life? About herself? About himself?

These are not the questions many parents are asking today. Instead, parents are feeling pressured to concentrate on preparing their children for a competitive world in which opportunities for success are shrinking and are linked to technological expertise. Parenting has become overly serious. Fun, joy, play, spontaneity, adventure, laughter, imagination and spirituality all sit in second place behind achievement, careers and economic potential. Tom Sawyer and Pippi Longstocking have been eclipsed by the computer. Parents are in danger of losing their psychological and spiritual balance. Mom and Dad need to ask the questions that connect them to the souls of their children. Our book will explore these questions.

Nurturing the souls of our children is not easy. My wife, Bonnie, and I have found that parenting can throw us off balance quickly. Today it's hard enough to keep yourself on track — add the responsibility of raising a number of little human beings, and the odds of losing your balance skyrockets.

Emotional and spiritual balance put us in the best position to nurture the souls of our children — the essence of intimacy between child and parent. Our awareness of our children's souls is the surest guide to raising them wisely and allowing them to develop their individual lives. Our awareness of their souls protects them and ourselves from overindulgence or neglect, the two extremes of unbalanced parenting.

Their awareness of their own souls helps them develop an internal strength of character so necessary for self-worth.

Like most parents, Bonnie and I didn't anticipate the complexity of raising children. We came to parenting late. I was in my 40s. Up to that point, raising children seemed fairly simple. We had come into contact with many families in our work. We had always figured the secret of parenting was avoiding the mistakes our parents had made and repeating the good things they had done. And if in doubt, there were shelves of books in the parenting section of the local bookstore.

When our own children came along, this logical approach didn't work. For one thing, our kids hadn't read the same books we had read. For another we kept thinking of Professor Henry Higgins' words in *My Fair Lady* about letting a woman (read "child") "in your life and your serenity is gone." We found being parents can leave you feeling inadequate, anxious and out of balance.

Eventually, we discovered how to meet the problems of parenthood and — at the same time — not miss its joys and fulfillment. The secret is keeping yourself psychologically and spiritually balanced. We have found this to be the single most important quality in raising our own children and in helping hundreds of families over our thirty-five years as counselors. When parents maintain their balance, the inevitable "curveballs" that children throw are easier to connect with. You may not hit a home run, but at least you won't strike out.

Our early lives began with an emphasis on the spiritual, myself as a priest, Bonnie as a religious sister. Although our paths hadn't crossed yet, individually we had become aware that our work with people was psychologically inadequate. After leaving the Religious Orders, we pursued careers in psychology. We were not yet wise enough to recognize the spiritual limitations of the field. That was to take a number of years living outside the monastery and convent as a couple and as parents.

After more than two decades of searching for ways to become better parents to our own children and more effective helpers to the families with whom we worked, we understand the necessity for a balance of the psychological and the spiritual. What we offer you in these pages are ways to maintain psychological and spiritual balance. These approaches put you in the best position to nurture the souls of your children. Our suggestions don't come only from academic theories. We've lived them. They have come from our earlier lives in religion, our twenty-five year marriage, and the raising of a daughter and a son. We've also drawn on our experiences of the last thirty-five years working with individuals, couples, and families to help them find meaning in their lives and repair their earlier emotional wounds.

We are grateful for the rich lessons we have learned from the many people who have touched our souls in our work, first as a Catholic priest and nun and then as a clinical psychologist and a Marriage Family Therapist. Witnessing their courage in overcoming their problems, we have become wiser.

We have been encouraged to put our ideas into print by the people who attend our talks. However, we aren't so presumptuous to think that our advice will fit everyone. It isn't the last word. Read what we have experienced with a critical eye. Take what looks useful. *Try it out.* See if it works for you.

We have arranged the topics much as we would a series of talks for parents. In fact, the basis for the chapters are the talks, workshops, seminars and retreats we have been giving for the last twenty-five years. You don't have to read this book starting at the first page. We've designed each chapter to be a self-contained unit.

We invite you to "drop in" on the topic(s) of your interest much like you would come on a given evening to one of our talks. Chapter I, *Keeping Your Balance,* describes psychological and spiritual balance. Chapter II, *Our Stories,* personalizes our journeys, giving you a brief glimpse into where Bonnie and I have been and where we are now. Chapter III, *Nurturing the Souls of Our Children,* is the core of our message. Parents who nurture the souls of their children give them a strong foundation for a good future. Chapter IV, *Affluenza: Are We Giving Our Children Too Much?* offers parents ways to protect the souls of their children from our materialistic, consumer-driven society. Chapter V, *Humor in the Family,* shares ideas to keep a better balance between the heavy and light sides of family life. Chapter VI, *Taking Charge in Your Home,* gives parents a chance to see "who's running the store." The souls of children flourish in a safe, secure environment. Chapter VII, *Eleven Guideposts on the Road to Balance,* maps out practical ways to stay on the path of psychological and spiritual balance that leads to nurturing the souls of our children.

We know that whenever we pick up a book on parenting, family, or ways of maturing, we often feel inadequate because what we read is an "ideal" description of life. The real world where we live is far from that. Think of these pages as a goal to aim for rather than a place where you should already be. Ted Williams was the last Major League baseball player to get a hit four times out of ten, and he is in baseball's Hall of Fame. Remember, *nobody* bats a thousand.

Neither psychology nor religion has an exclusive lock on the intricate and mysterious process called *life.* Psychology has much to offer about the dynamics of human behavior, the effects of childhood on adult functioning, differences between the sexes, the origins of self-defeating choices, addictions, and many other areas of life. But it is less clear about the deeper mysteries of life, death, what happens after death, loss of a loved one, the existence of God, terminal illness, evil, and the meaning of life that spirituality addresses.

This book offers useful ways to maintain a family's balance. We present some of the time-honored wisdom passed down through the ages from the worlds of psychology and spirituality. We have tried to make it relevant for today's parents. For many years, these issues have been the main focus of our lives.

In our opinion, a genuine psychological search is necessarily spiritual. Dogma or a specific set of religious doctrine plays a secondary role in becoming spiritually balanced. Our experience is that God pays attention to us individually, guiding us through life's challenges. God's connection is not limited to special denominations. Spirituality is a vital part of being human.

It is our hope that you will find in these pages the help to create a balanced psychological and spiritual environment for your family. We believe this dual awareness is what's missing from the books we've seen on raising children. We have read books that talk about the psychological aspects of parenting without mentioning the spiritual. We have also found many books that rely almost exclusively on the spiritual, omitting what we have learned from the findings of psychology.

We hope these pages help both to keep you grounded in the psychological and spiritual and enable you to nurture the soul of your child.

CHAPTER I

Keeping Your Balance

The new postmodern family is more flexible, more permeable, more urbane, but also out of balance because it fails to meet the needs of children.

David Elkind
Ties That Stress

In the early 1970s, I came back to the U.S. after working as a missionary priest in Peru for eight years. The first thing that struck me was the pet food ads on television. Frolicking cats and dogs were romping through lush green yards, their glistening fur and boundless energy a proof of the care they were getting from the smiling owners who sang the praises of the advertised pet food.

In the abject poverty of the *Barriadas* (slums) of Lima, the *Favelas* of Rio de Janeiro, and the *Altiplano* of Bolivia, I had seen people near starvation. The wide-eyed, vacant expression on the faces of starving children had burned an indelible image in my mind. To me something seemed out of balance with well-fed animals on the one hand and hungry men, women and children on the other.

The last few years I've been getting the feeling that many people are out of balance. Bonnie and I watch the media bombard families with messages of instant gratification. In commercials, people appear happy, contented and fulfilled all because they've bought one of the endless variety of advertised products. At the same time, however, we don't hear many offsetting voices that speak to our children's deeper human and spiritual sides, that speak of their souls. Because of this, we feel the need to encourage parents to get back on track psychologically and spiritually in order to nourish the souls of their children.

Something is wrong. We've all felt that. Modern life seems to have "jumped the track." At the many talks Bonnie and I give, we find people are trying to be good parents, but they don't know how to bring their families back into balance. They sense something is off with many of the values that society is espousing. For example, some well-known actors are casually portraying smoking cigarettes as "cool." Yet we have overwhelming evidence of cigarettes' deadly effects and of the powerful influence of movies on viewers, especially children. Sports heroes and a sprinkling of Hollywood glitterati give the message that cigar smoking is "in," unaware, or worse, unconcerned that young people eagerly follow their lead.

Some in the media use our precious first amendment rights to pump out gratuitous sex and inappropriate violence without considering their effects on youth. Parents need the knowledge and skills to deal with these modern problems in raising their children. Parents need to know how to make good choices to protect their children without going to an extreme and making them overly fearful and suspicious of society. In order to make wise choices, parents have to stay balanced psychologically and spiritually.

There Balance Is Missing

Balance is missing in parents whose kids have become selfish and ungrateful, even though they have been given so much, whose teenagers believe they are totally in charge of their own lives, and whose children refuse to do homework because it's unpleasant. Balance is missing in parents who say they can no longer control their four-year-olds, and whose ten-year-olds become alcoholics. It is missing in marriages where the only positive connection between the parents is the children, in families that seldom talk to each other, in parents who are more connected to their children's achievements than to their souls, and in divorces where parents use the children as weapons against each other. Balance is missing in the parent who uses his child as a confidant, and, most tragically, in families whose children run away or think seriously of suicide.

There are two kinds of balance that we have to develop: psychological and spiritual. Neither one by itself is enough to truly nurture the souls of our children. Psychological and spiritual balance are two sides of the same coin, are interwoven pieces of the same fabric, are two halves forming a whole. To exaggerate one is to diminish the other. As parents, we need to pay equal importance to and understand both if we want to nurture the souls of our children.

Psychological Balance

Psychological balance is not a permanent state of mind. It comes and goes. There are times when balanced adults feel more grounded, and times when they feel utterly lost and at sea. Sometimes it's admitting the feeling of being lost and at sea that is the proof of balance. Generally, the balanced adult is simply more balanced than not, which is all any of us can ever hope to be.

It takes years of experience with both success and failure before we can establish the priorities that make for a balanced life. That you have to be a mature adult to be psychologically balanced is hardly a new idea. Plato didn't think a person could be in charge of others until mid-life. He thought a few years under your belt was a necessary teacher.

Balanced people are not often thrown off track for long. When something upsetting happens, a balanced person usually recovers before he or she does something self-destructive or harmful to others, even though the urge to strangle is intense. My sister and brother-in-law, who have ten children, came home from an overnight trip to find that their fifteen-year-old daughter had driven the family station wagon into the side of the house, ripping out a sizeable portion of stucco and smashing the fender beyond repair. In their absence, she had decided to practice backing out of the driveway. They found the culprit shaking and crying, too frightened to talk or even to look them in the eye. My brother-in-law, who with ten kids could write a book about upsetting experiences, put his arm around his daughter and gently told her he was happy she wasn't hurt, that the car and house could always be repaired. Here was a balanced parent showing good judgment by nurturing his daughter's troubled soul rather than punishing her already-crushed spirit. He knew blunders are part of life.

At a workshop we were giving for school directors on psychological and spiritual balance, one of them told us that her infant son had died from crib death some years before. Whenever something unusually upsetting happens, she said, her husband keeps her grounded by whispering, "Nobody's dying here."

It's not easy to keep our balance, especially as parents. Our children don't usually give us advance notice about their actions. Your preteen doesn't call you up at work and say, "Dad, I want to let you know that at 8:00 tonight I'm going to pull something that will drive you crazy." Or, your toddler doesn't warn you that in fifteen minutes she's going to throw a tantrum. It's always a surprise. I know I've gone from the tenderest of thoughts toward my kids to near-homicidal feelings in less than ten seconds.

It's a struggle to pull yourself back to the center, back to balance, back to where the soul resides. Tom, a chaplain friend of mine, described this struggle when he said, "Keeping your balance today takes a lot of energy since you have to hold the two extremes equally distant from you. It's like controlling the reins of two wild horses." Most parents know what he means.

The artist Louise Bourgeois also talks about balance as the fragile center between two extremes. We are pulled between the incessant demands of parenting and the need for a life of our own. It's only by keeping an appropriate balance between these two extremes that we are able to develop psychologically and spiritually, and, thereby, be capable of nurturing the souls of our children.

Spiritual Balance

We believe spiritually-balanced people have four characteristics: 1) they ponder the deeper questions of life like death, serious illness, suffering, evil, the meaning of life, and life after death; 2) they consider others as important as themselves; 3) they connect to a cause or belief that recognizes a power greater than the self; and 4) they experience a genuine inner peace.

Psychology focuses on making our lives run smoothly so we can avoid conflicts within ourselves and with others. There is even some common ground between spirituality and psychology since both address human suffering, resilience and change. However, the emphasis of psychology is on eliminating the symptoms that cause our lives to be unsatisfying. For example, communication skills are taught to couples or to parents and children who don't understand each other. Clinical depression is sometimes treated by medication to lessen the severity of the symptoms, along with psychotherapy to find self-fulfilling ways to deal with life.

On the other hand, spirituality focuses on what meaning my life will have had as an individual, a spouse, or a parent when I have to face death. Is there a purpose or plan to the sixty, seventy or more years I'll be alive? How do I find meaning in a serious illness — my own or a loved one's? Psychology prepares us to become better students of life.

Spirituality makes us philosophers — to make sense out of life and death. Years ago the singer Peggy Lee caused many people to think about their lives with the song, "Is that all there is, my friend?"

The second characteristic of spiritually-balanced people is recognizing they are not the center of the world. Psychology emphasizes the development of the self. Words like self-worth, self-esteem, self-actualization, individuation, and independence are buzzwords in the world of psychology. Some people take this search to the extreme.

Spirituality turns the obsessive search for the self on its heels. Spirituality lingers in paradoxes. It sees wisdom in the following: only by losing the self can a person find himself and his soul; the more you learn the less you know; the more you give to others the richer you are; the first shall be last and the last shall be first.

Spirituality connects us to others. Their need is as important to us as ours is. "Do unto others as you would have them do unto you." And "Love your neighbor as yourself" are good guidelines for people who are searching for spiritual balance. Nor is there any need to put others down or to be first all the time. Our modern obsession with being "number one" is a sad, yet graphic symptom of the absence of spirituality today.

We have also noticed that spiritually balanced people almost inevitably turn their attention to the needs of children. They see children as both vulnerable and as the hope of the future. They are willing to make sacrifices to ensure children have a brighter future.

Thirdly, spiritually-balanced people have a sense of security in life. This quality grows out of their ability to lean confidently on a power or cause greater than the self. They feel part of a plan, which gives meaning to their lives. There is great relief from believing your life has a purpose — that your life is linked and even guided by a higher power. This is what the spiritual *He's Got the Whole World in His Hands* conveys.

Bonnie and I can only explain our involvement in the work we do by some power outside ourselves. We set out to distance ourselves from the spiritual by emphasizing the psychological. Yet, now we are passionately urging modern families to integrate the spiritual with the psychological in nurturing the souls of their children.

Finally, spiritually-balanced people are more relaxed. They don't take themselves too seriously. They can laugh at themselves. They feel comfortable with themselves. They don't have unrealistic expectations of others or of themselves. They are not easily thrown off track by the latest fad. They are reflective and wise. As far as possible, they have made some sense out of their lives. They see good more powerful than evil. They accept tragedy, grief, and death as part of life. They are joyful. They are resilient. They are at peace.

Our Children's Legacy

We want to pass on balanced values to our children, not "just" a large estate. Bonnie and I have been giving talks to parents from all walks of life and every religion as well as to corporate groups which profess no religious beliefs. What we've seen is a quiet revolution growing, spearheaded by parents who are turning away from the unbalanced focus of making money first, last and only that ruled the 80s and early 90s. These parents have stepped off the bottom line to take matters into their own hands. They have accepted the fact that they cannot rely on the media, movies, professional sports, nor even completely on the government and churches to provide leadership and guidance in raising children. These parents are no longer content to simply complain; they are actively searching for solutions.

Grieshog

Frequently parents ask Bonnie and me about how to keep their balance in a world that has lost its moral compass. When we try to frame an answer, we're reminded of the Irish custom of *Grieshog*. This is an Irish word that means to put ashes over the burning hearth coals at night to keep the fire alive. In the morning, the people brushed aside the ashes and added new fuel to the still-hot coals to stoke the fire up for the new day's warmth and cooking.

We see this same phenomenon happening among parents. For the last fifteen or twenty years, society has "grieshogged" the deeper psychological and spiritual values under the ashes of self-centered materialism. Now parents are looking for ways to brush aside those ashes and are looking for ways to stoke up the warmth in the smoldering fire of human souls hidden below. Timothy encourages us to "Fan into flame the gifts you were given." (1:6)

Last year a group of twenty parents approached us worried that the unrelenting exposure their children were getting from TV commercialism and media violence might be damaging. They explained that their dilemma was how to protect their kids from the exposure yet still teach them how to deal with real life — to love life rather than fear it. We set up a series of meetings at which my wife and I laid out much of what you're reading now. At the end of the series, they told us that they no longer felt overwhelmed. They felt they had acquired what they needed to create the balanced family environment they'd been searching for. It is our hope that you will become better balanced after reading these pages. And, in keeping your balance, you'll be more capable of nurturing the souls of your children.

CHAPTER II

Our Stories

We are now more aware that faith and grace are life processes, the very heart of that life process we call 'maturation.' God expects us to grow up — that has been the message of revelation from at least as far back as Jeremiah. We are meant to be decisive and self-determining. We are meant to develop a distinctive self-identity. We cannot be blessed by God for handing over to others in blind submission those choices that are demanded by the circumstances of our lives . . . I must become a mature lover, I must become free. I must discover the truth of myself and of the world around me.

Bernard Cooke

Tom's Story

I spent many years expecting authority figures to make society better. Finally, I reached the conclusion that each of us can do a lot of good in our own small world whether the institutions we belong to are ready to join in or not.

For many of those years, I lived in an institutional world. I entered the Carmelite Catholic seminary in Niagara Falls, Canada. The Carmelite Religious Order is known for its emphasis on spirituality and prayer. Besides engaging in all forms of church ministry, its members live communally in monasteries. For eleven years, I trained in the predominately spiritual aspects of life. After my ordination as a Catholic priest, I spent six years on the south side of Chicago teaching at an all-boys high school, while doing parish work on weekends.

After many years of theory, it was exciting to be in the trenches dealing with people's everyday problems. I quickly learned, however, how naïve I was. The human problems my textbooks described were quite different from the conflicts struggling people faced daily.

During the late 50s and early 60s in Catholic seminaries, priests were trained in a catechetical approach, a method that offered ready solutions to many human problems. With some embarrassment, I now look back and see how inadequate many of these "canned" answers were. I sometimes think that if hell exists and I find myself there, my punishment will be to listen to my old sermons.

While teaching high school, I completed a Master's Degree in Education from the University of Chicago. Although I didn't realize it at the time, my own sense of being unbalanced was awakening. I had naïvely thought that good people were necessarily connected to a church — especially my own. But the selfless, dedicated, non-religious people I met at the University forced me to rethink my assumptions.

I met a man who had spent a number of years in China as a Protestant missionary. He had come back to the U.S. to reconsider his commitment to China. He told me that if he were to go back, he knew it would be for life. He felt that he would need to sever all ties to this country and become a Chinese citizen in order to identify with the people with whom he worked. At the end of our degree program, he decided to return. I struggled for a long time with my belief that you had to be Catholic to be that holy; yet that man was — and still is — one of the two most genuinely spiritual persons I've ever known. The other was a Carmelite priest who was my superior early in my training. Since my non-Catholic missionary friend didn't fit my mold, I had to look my bias straight in the eye.

Partly from adventure and, perhaps, partly from his example, I volunteered for missionary work in South America. I spent from 1961 to 1969 in Lima, Peru. At that time we American missionaries saw our task as exposing the Peruvians to the efficient, activity-centered American Catholic Church. To Peruvians we Yankee missionaries were so efficient and organized that they told the story, tongue-in-cheek, of an American factory where a live pig could be put on a conveyor belt at one end, run through various machines and come out at the other end as packaged pork chops, bacon and ham. If there were no buyers, the finished products were simply run back through the machine, and the live pig reappeared.

To my surprise, this kind of efficiency just didn't appeal to my Peruvian parishioners. They were quite content not to be slaves to the clock. They valued tradition. They savored the moment. They forced me to reexamine my own basic assumptions. Watching people who didn't take rules too seriously, I began to question my legalistic, impersonal approach to religion. I began to wonder why they seemed to have a more intimate relationship with God, and to be better balanced than I. I envied how they enjoyed life while I was continually focused on achieving goals.

Every year I spent in Peru, I felt more strongly that the advice I was giving to people was inadequate. One incident brought this home to me. A young couple whose precious six-year-old daughter drowned in a neighbor's swimming pool asked me why God permitted such a tragedy. She had been pulled out of the water a few hours before. Since bodies are not embalmed in Peru, the burial takes place within twenty-four hours. We were in the child's bedroom. Her stuffed animals and tiny knick-knacks still cluttered the top of her dresser. Her child-like drawings decorated the walls. On the nightstand was a picture of the little girl smiling and holding hands with a friend. Laid out on her bed, she looked like she was sleeping peacefully. I recall the intensity in the tearful eyes of this despairing couple as they searched my face for something to help them comprehend what had happened. My words about our not knowing the will of God and how God writes straight in crooked lines felt hollow and insensitive. The abrupt exposure of my inadequacy felt like being stripped naked before them.

I was in Lima on Tuesday, November 27, 1962, when a Varig Brazilian airplane with ninety-seven passengers on board crashed into the desolate, sand-colored mountains at Jorge Chavez International Airport a few miles outside the city of Lima. The pilot was told to make a turn because of its altitude and because an Air France flight was about to take off. The Brazilian airplane turned the wrong way. All ninety-seven passengers were killed. Thirty-seven of them were Peruvians, a number were from my parish. For two days, I went from house to house of the families of the victims. A few of the homes were large, with Spanish style balconies overlooking enclosed courtyards paved with multicolored tiles. However, most of the homes were modest, one-story houses of the rising middle class. The size of the home made no difference as each family tried to cope with the catastrophe. As their priest I brought the comforts of the rituals of their religion. Yet I was unable to contain my own grief, even as I tried to explain the unexplainable to the despondent loved ones. Nothing in my training or in my experience had prepared me for this. I seemed to be drowning in an ocean of grief.

Another tragedy left me feeling even more out of balance. On May 24, 1964, there was an important soccer match between Peru and Argentina at the National Stadium of Lima. *Futbol* in South America is an intense national sport. When an Uruguayan referee annulled a Peruvian goal, a riot broke out. In the melee thousands of fans rushed for the exits and found the giant steel doors bolted shut. Those reaching the exit doors first were crushed and suffocated by the thrust of the panic-filled people behind them. I had just finished saying an evening Mass and was removing the liturgical vestments in the church sacristy, when several people burst in with the news of the catastrophe. I vividly recall the reports of the mounting number of fatalities. First ten, then twenty, then forty. A growing group of shocked parishioners joined me as I went back into the church to pray the Rosary for the victims. Breathless, despondent people kept interrupting our prayers with frightening announcements of an ever increasing number of dead until we heard the confirmed number of three hundred.

Three of the dead were personal friends. One, a well-educated business man of about forty-five, had studied in the U.S. He knew the American culture very well. He had been a great help to me in explaining those facets of the Peruvian culture that I had found difficult to understand. For instance, he pointed out that Peruvians saw us Americans as somewhat tactless when we responded directly and bluntly to a request we could not fulfill. "On the contrary," he said, "we Peruvians are concerned with how the person will feel. We respond indirectly and slowly. In this way, we show respect so that when we finally have to decline the request or pass on the bad news, the person has been strengthened by our sensitivity." This bit of advice helped me enormously. I would miss him very much.

The other two, a married couple in their late thirties, had frequently volunteered to work on parish committees. We had become close friends. They had welcomed me into their family, and I felt like an uncle to their five young children. My choked words to their family, especially to the five children, could not comfort me, either. I was ill-equipped to deal with what I now know was posttraumatic stress syndrome among the families who looked to me for help. I began to realize I needed to develop another dimension of my own soul for which my priesthood training had not prepared me.

In 1970, I returned to the U.S. and decided to resign from the Carmelites. At that time, members of a Religious Order took a vow of poverty which meant that personally we owned nothing. The down side of that psychologically is that we were spared from the ordinary financial worries that most adults face like adequate salaries, mortgages, car loans, medical bills and, eventually, raising children. I realized I had depended heavily on an institution to support and protect me financially and emotionally. Now, I felt I had to make my own way in life. I knew it would not be easy. Like a young man leaving his family, I had to discover my own world apart from the protecting arms of the Church.

After trying my hand, unsuccessfully, as a social worker and a life insurance salesperson, I eventually got a part-time job as an adult school teacher for the Los Angeles City School District. This enabled me to attend the California School of Professional Psychology in Los Angeles. Three years later, I had a Ph.D. in clinical psychology and the naïve idea that I would now find all the missing pieces of life.

Much of what I learned in my psychological studies was very helpful in understanding the emotional and mental makeup of people. Yet I soon began to see that the deeper questions about life, death, pain, suffering, and loss were inadequately addressed by psychology alone. While I had found deficiencies in theology to deal with some human problems, I now found deficiencies in psychology to deal with spiritual concerns. I began to feel a need for the answers and beliefs of my priesthood. What I had previously seen as vague, lifeless words took on fresh meaning now that I had a psychological framework to fit them into. And once I blended my spiritual beliefs into my studies, my psychological insights took on more significance. I began, at last, to experience what real human balance was.

I didn't always find balance in the world of psychology. Some of my psychology professors and students demeaned religion. They viewed religious expression through the negative experiences of their own childhood.

For example, in Metropolitan State Psychiatric Hospital, near Los Angeles, I witnessed a psychiatrist and a psychologist teasing a twenty-two-year-old schizophrenic patient about his belief that God intervenes directly in our lives. "Do you think God will help me fix my car or show me which horse to bet on?" one doctor asked him. I vividly recall the wide-eyed look of panic on the gaunt face of this vulnerable patient. The young man's eyes filled with fear. Blood drained from his face. He looked like a frightened fawn caught in the glaring headlights of a hunter's car. I can still hear their mocking voices stripping him of what little comfort he had. Whatever therapeutic method that was supposed to be, it wasn't balanced. Balanced people don't attack a helpless person's beliefs for their own enjoyment.

Later, I talked to the young man about his belief in God. He told me God was his only friend, the only one who really understood him. I was touched by his words. I felt whatever tenuous tie he had with reality, it had much to do with his belief in the divine. Psychiatry could help control his hallucinations and delusions. It could even teach him to live in society. But only his spiritual beliefs calmed the raging waters of his insanity.

It was this and similar experiences that taught me that psychiatric and psychological interventions were often inadequate to bring about a balance in a patient's life unless there was also a spiritual component to the treatment. In some cases the spiritual component needed to be rooted in a specific religious doctrine. In others it was simply connected to a belief in a higher power.

Unfortunately, the attitudes I saw at Metropolitan Hospital weren't unusual in the field. I moved on to my internship in a Community Free Clinic. As part of our training, we interns had to attend "group supervision." This included talking about the patients each of us were seeing and sharing with the group the emotional impact each patient had upon us. The group supervisor, a clinical psychologist, demanded that each group participant bare his/her soul. If he wasn't satisfied with the emotional depth of an intern, he would call the offending student demeaning names. Standing an inch from the offender's ear, he would scream profanities like an old-time Marine drill sergeant, until the person broke down. Finally, in the middle of one of his tirades against a young male intern of about twenty-five, I felt compelled, as the senior in the group, to stand up and tell the supervisor he was cruel and unprofessional. He dropped me from the group as a result, but, at least, I felt I brought a moment of balance to the beleaguered interns.

Still, I had to admit that religion doesn't guarantee balance either. Balance is an internal process not necessarily connected to religious expertise. I had a seminary professor who was a hypochondriac. When you had to hand in a test and knew you hadn't done very well, you walked directly up to the professor to hand him your completed exam, making a point to cough and sneeze on the paper. He would step back as if he had stumbled upon a coiled rattlesnake about to strike, a shocked look on his face, his hand frozen in mid-air, fingers extended as if to repel mortal danger. "Put it on the desk," he'd hiss. You knew he wouldn't touch your paper much less correct it.

I can't judge this priest too harshly. As a twenty-seven-year-old celibate, I once taught a course to nurses at a local Catholic hospital, in which I explained at length what husbands and wives needed to do to have a successful marriage. Fortunately for me, the nurses were merciful. I saw them choke down laughter more than once, but they never asked me any tough questions, even when I pontificated about the sexual nature of marriage. My only hope, recalling my lectures, is that they have short memories. If not, they probably have a few good stories about my words of wisdom at their reunions.

I don't mean to imply that priests and nuns don't help many people. They do. I can attest to that. I've worked alongside selfless, dedicated priests and nuns in the United States and in South America. However, as with all caretakers, their capacity to help is greatly affected by their psychological and spiritual balance. Nobody can give what he hasn't got.

Psychological balance includes making mistakes just as spiritual balance includes not doing the right thing all the time. We develop personal insight from our blunders, and humility from our sins. Daniel Levinson, in his classic work on midlife, tells us we can only become psychologically balanced by admitting we have both helped and harmed others. He describes it as accepting the creative and destructive part in each of us. It's not avoiding but embracing the negative part of us that keeps us balanced. A perfectionist is as unbalanced as a ne'er-do-well. Neither accepts himself fully: one can't stand himself when he fails; the other when he succeeds.

Gene, a fifty-five-year-old father of two grown children, had to face the painful fact that, at one period of his life, he had neglected his children. The alcoholic behavior of his wife had played a major part, but still, he had to admit he was also responsible for his own choices. He hadn't done enough to protect his children from the alcoholism of his wife. He had thrown himself into his work and had let them deal with her erratic behavior. He went to his children, now parents of their own children, and openly apologized. He neither excused nor defended himself. He and his children were then able to see the creative things Gene had done for them once he was free to admit the destructive ones. Gene became better balanced.

Jim had a problem with his brother-in-law since the first day they met. Jim saw him as insensitive, abrupt, unapproachable, and divisive. Furthermore, most of Jim's family shared his opinion. One day Jim shared his thoughts and feelings with a family member who promptly told the brother-in-law. What had been a cold, distant relationship now became hostile. When Jim related the situation to more discreet family members, they said, "Well, you only told the truth," or, "It's not your fault he's such a pain in the neck."

Despite the reassurances, Jim could not quell the little voice within him saying, "Apologize." He wrestled with himself for weeks. He rationalized, *Any apology would be wasted. He deserved it. He'll never like me no matter what I do.*

Like a wheel off track — like having a small pebble in his shoe — Jim felt out of balance. No matter what the justifying reasons were, he was responsible for causing harm to another person. He knew he had to apologize without any strings attached, like expecting their relationship to improve or hoping his brother-in-law would think better of him.

The whole extended family came together for Thanksgiving. A moment came when his brother-in-law was sitting alone. *Now or never,* Jim said to himself. He went over, sat down directly in front of the man, and looking him squarely in the eye said simply, "I'm sorry for what I said. I had no right to say those things."

Their relationship has not improved. Jim never knew whether his brother-in-law ever told anyone in the family. Nevertheless, Jim felt a great burden released as he regained his balance by acknowledging the destructive part of himself.

I have surely made my share of mistakes. One of my more serious incidents of causing pain happened within my own family. My aunt's pastor told her she couldn't attend her son's second wedding because he was divorced. She asked my opinion. Forty years later, the memory of my agreeing with the pastor continues to haunt me. I can still feel her sorrowful, uncomprehending eyes riveted on me as I failed to respond to a mother's human request. One more awkward step toward the middle on the ladder of balance — Sigh!

Bonnie recalls that as a young nun teaching elementary school, she used to wonder why some of her students' mothers did not volunteer more time to help in the school and parish. After all, they were home all day. It wasn't until she became a mother that she learned to understand the hectic, unpredictable life mothers have. She was a stay-at-home mom until our children were in school and remembers how her blood boiled when remarks were made about the soft life of "non-working moms." Now, she recognizes that such comments and her earlier viewpoint came from psychological imbalance.

Bonnie's Story

I grew up in a Catholic environment. In 1961, immediately after high school, I entered the convent. I was seventeen. The Order I chose was the Immaculate Heart Community of Religious Sisters in Los Angeles, an Order open to the latest thinking in theology, sociology and philosophy. As a result, I received an excellent education and was exposed to many cultural experiences in music, film and art. One example of the high quality of the faculty was the internationally-known artist Corita Kent, who was head of the art department.

The Community encouraged its members to go on for higher education. All offices were open to those qualified. I learned, within the confines of this group the sky was the limit for women. There were no men. I felt free of the male cultural dominance in the larger society.

The General Council of the Catholic Church, called Vatican II, had challenged religious communities to look at themselves psychologically, socially and culturally and to make revisions in their rules to fit the times. But there was a struggle in some Religious Orders whether to modernize or to continue with the long-established traditions. My Order chose to move in a new direction, even at the cost of having its official status removed by Church authorities. We were asked to nullify our vows of poverty, chastity and obedience. Those who decided to remain committed themselves to the newly-formed Immaculate Heart Community, which continues to this day as a lay group.

I feel fortunate to have belonged to such a courageous association of women who chose a whole new direction as a result of their evolving convictions. However, it was time for me to explore new options like a new career, marriage and having children. I decided to leave in 1969.

It was not an easy decision. I questioned if I could make it "on my own." The Order had assumed all financial responsibility for me as my parents had before. I had never faced the ordinary decisions other young adults were used to making: buying a car, renting an apartment, obtaining insurance, facing the future in the work force, and balancing a budget. This challenge seemed both exciting and frightening.

I had to face a less-protected world than I had known. One sobering incident forced me to deal with a grim reality of life that now, I see, strengthened me. I was teaching adult night school in East Los Angeles in the early '70s. One night I stayed after class to help several students and so was late coming out of the school building. Since it was dark and the parking lot almost empty, I ran to my car. While driving home, I began to notice an increasing number of police cars behind me. Then I thought I heard a helicopter hovering above. I remember saying to myself, *They must be after somebody big.*

As I pulled off the freeway heading for my apartment, I was almost blinded by an intense bright, flashing light shining into my car. I heard a booming voice say, "You, lady, in the white Mercury, pull over NOW."

I said out loud, "My God, that's MY car. They're after ME."

Frightened and shaking, I pulled my car over to the shoulder and stopped. Police scrambled up on both sides of my car with guns drawn, pointing at me. One officer yelled at me to put down the window and keep my hands on the steering wheel. I told them I was a teacher and was about to reach over to the passenger side to show him my role book. The officer stuck his gun in the window close to my head and said, "Keep your hands on the wheel! Do you want me to shoot you?"

There had been a bomb threat at the school, and the area was under police surveillance. When they saw me running to my car with no one else around, the police suspected I was the bomber. After ten frantic minutes of pleading with the police to let me show them my teacher's role book, I finally convinced them I was not the bomber. It was a baptism of fire in the unprotected, real world. That night I realized that in my search for psychological development, I had to give up the protection of the convent.

I enjoyed teaching. However, I soon realized that what interested me was the psychological aspects of the students' growth in addition to their educational development. I was in charge of an experimental program for disadvantaged young adults, which gave me the opportunity to combine their academics with psychological growth. While I felt my religious formation had not equipped me sufficiently to deal with peoples' psychological problems, I now saw that for me educational approaches were also lacking in this area. I quickly realized I was ill-prepared to deal with the underlying emotional problems that kept many of my otherwise bright, talented students from succeeding.

One of them was Irene, a beautiful young woman of twenty. She had dropped out of high school in her senior year and, now, had entered our program with the hope of getting her high school diploma. Irene was bright, articulate, a leader and a promising young writer. She was a joy to teach.

As the weeks went by, I noticed she started missing class, failing to hand in her assignments and withdrawing from the group. I spoke to her and offered my help. But, I became aware she needed more than educational guidance and encouragement. What had kept her from succeeding earlier in high school was still not resolved. She dropped out of the program. I never heard from her again. I still think of her and others like her whom I met in that special program. After the program ended, I knew I wanted to pursue a career in psychology.

I met Tom in 1971. We married in 1973. Our daughter was born in 1975 and our son in 1977. I left teaching and became a part-time student in the graduate psychology program at California State University, Northridge. At the same time, with our two young children in preschool, I was immersed in a world of mothers. Preschool moms spend a lot of time together. I saw them struggling to have some sense of their own identity as well as trying to understand their relationships with their children and husbands. They were caught in the varied, and often conflicting, roles of mother, wife, daughter, friend and volunteer. Many seemed to feel that no matter how hard they tried, they always came up short. Many had little sense of themselves apart from these roles. Some felt out-of-step with the new emphasis on careers for women because they wanted to stay at home and be with their children. Others felt guilty because they wanted to devote more time to their careers. Still others were struggling because they had to work to support the family. I sensed they were out of balance. I had to face my own difficult choice of putting my professional goals on hold to spend more time with my children. I compromised by going to graduate school part-time. It took me five years to complete a two-year program.

As part of the academic counseling program, we were encouraged to enter our own psychotherapy. With the help of a compassionate Jewish analyst, I was able to examine the unworked-out issues in my life, those which had kept me unbalanced. This relationship proved to be an important factor in my search for psychological and spiritual balance. It showed me how human and spiritual connections are deeper than those based solely on religious denominational ties. Here was a Jewish male guiding me to a greater understanding of myself and of my relationships with others.

Where I had previously felt unprepared to deal with psychological issues as a nun, I now discovered a lack of spiritual balance in some of my psychological training. It was not uncommon to hear remarks made in class and lectures by both students and professionals about religion, spirituality or peoples' faith — comments seemingly based upon ignorance and bias. At one lecture, I remember several students blaming organized religion for most of the world's problems — and the professor wholeheartedly agreeing. My objection that this was stereotyping and therefore an unbalanced view of religion was met with stony silence. Later on Tom and I would try to raise the consciousness of mental health professionals regarding the value of religious belief in the overall mental health of patients. We spoke at the annual conventions of the California State Psychological Association and the Marriage, Family and Child Therapists' Convention on the positive use of the religious belief of patients in the psychotherapy process.

When I finished my degree program, the same feeling of wanting to help others that had led me to become a nun returned. This time it was a belief that I could shepherd women, especially mothers, to a clearer sense of themselves. I knew that a large part of my work as a professional counselor would be in women's issues, running mother-to-mother and women's journey groups. My earlier experiences in the Order and in therapy helped me in my own continual struggle toward psychological and spiritual balance, so I felt uniquely prepared to guide them on their own psychological and spiritual journeys.

Tom and I have seen in our lives a guiding hand that has, almost without our knowing it, helped us clarify our life's goal — to help families get into better psychological and spiritual balance. Our early intense spiritual formation as nun and priest followed by our equally intense psychological formation has convinced us that true human balance comes from a foundation that is grounded equally in the spiritual and in the psychological.

CHAPTER III

Nurturing the Souls
of Our Children

If I had but two loaves of bread, I would sell one and buy
hyacinths, for they would feed my soul.

The Koran

I've been going to the same gas station for the past five years. Close to my home, the neighborhood station has eight islands for self-serve and one for full-serve. Like most of my neighbors, I use the self-serve — it's cheaper. Usually I arrive around 7:00 a.m. and find most of the pumps in use. I recognize most of the faces — they're my neighbors. Yet, though we're all involved in the same ritual, there is no eye contact. No smiles, no good mornings. We don't even talk to an attendant! The whole process is computerized. Just put your credit card in the slot. It occurs to me afresh each time that the machine is the only one here who knows my name. Each time it greets me, *Welcome, Thomas F. Geary.* No voice, just amber words on a black screen. Wouldn't it be a nice touch if once in a while the message read, *Hi, Tom. How's the family?*

And that's the problem. *Machines don't make human connections. Machines don't nurture our souls.* As society becomes increasingly tech-oriented, we are losing the ability to reach out to each other in a personal way. Machines are replacing us in our daily interactions with each other. We have blurred the line that divides machines and people. Several weeks ago, at my office, I answered the phone myself instead of letting my voice mail fill in for me. The caller turned out to be a good friend who has known me for twenty years. Yet, when I said, "Hello, this is Dr. Geary," he didn't answer — he was waiting for the beep. It took several confused seconds — and as many "hellos" from me before he realized he was hearing *me.* It's an incident that typifies what's happened to us. Faceless people converse with each other on the Internet. Disembodied voices establish pseudo-friendships on talk radio. We feel "close" to celebrities who have no idea of who we are. The increasing lack of face-to-face contact disconnects us from each other. We are losing touch with each other's souls. We are missing our children's souls in the process.

What Is the Soul?

Soul is the deepest part of ourselves. It's the part that makes each of us an individual, distinct from every other individual. Science may be able to clone a body, but it will never be able to clone a soul. We can know what the soul is, but any attempt to describe it falls short. We define things by labeling them, by putting them in a box. Defining is our attempt to understand and control our world. Soul resists definitions. We can't pin the soul down with a fixed meaning. We cannot accurately and fully define soul because it resists boundaries. It can't be controlled. It can't be measured.

The soul embraces all facets of our life: past, present, and future; successes and failures; personality, temperament, character; hope; dreams; fantasies; loves and hates; tastes; fears; joys; humor; sexuality; struggles; what we are confused about; what we are sure of; our relationships (including to God if we so believe); and our thoughts about ourselves apart from the expectations of others.

The soul is not the same as personality or temperament. Personality refers to a relatively consistent way of behaving, feeling and thinking that makes one person different from another. For example, we talk about a quiet person as an introvert whereas an outgoing person is an extrovert. Temperament is a relatively predictable way a person reacts emotionally or approaches new situations. Some people tend to be optimistic (glass half full); others tend to be pessimistic (glass half empty).

The soul is more than intelligence. Intelligence is for analyzing, measuring, fact finding, memorizing, problem solving, and understanding complexities. Unfortunately today, some parents put too much stock in their child's intellectual "stats" since they seem to promise the greatest chance of getting into prestigious universities and attaining high-income careers. In our talks to parents, Bonnie and I describe how parents are no longer satisfied with merely gifted children; now the kids have to be "highly gifted." While we say this tongue-in-cheek, the reality is that this often unreal expectation puts enormous pressure on parents and children alike. Needless to say, it threatens the balance of their family.

In the twenty-five years I've been a psychologist, I've never once read a study of the soul. Psychology doesn't know quite what to do with this concept of soul which forces us to look more deeply at spiritual questions like suffering, death, life after death, the existence of God, the existence of evil, and the meaning of life.

In theological terms, soul is the purest form of God's creation, made in His/Her image and likeness. Being immeasurable, it most closely reflects the divine essence of God. "So God created human beings, making them to be like Himself." (Genesis 1:27) Soul is where all the profound values of a person reside, like loyalty, faith, hope, respect, commitment, responsibility, joy, and love. It is where we make our moral decisions. When you're in touch with your soul, you have the fullest possible picture of yourself; you're close to the divine. God doesn't see us in time frames (child, adult, old age); He/She doesn't know us more or less. God sees all of our life and knows us to the depths of our being at once and forever. God knows our soul.

On a human level, parents have the task of knowing the soul of each of their children as profoundly as possible. We are awash in a sea of numbers that measure the worth of our children's academic, athletic, and earning potential. Our heads are spinning with facts while our hearts are neglected. It is our heart that nurtures the souls of our children.

Every kind of human contact, intellectual, emotional and sensual, touches our souls. You need to see my eyes, hear my voice, touch my hand, and even, at some primal level, become aware of my scent to begin to know my soul. Sadly, the art of touching each other's souls is practically non-existent today. We've lost our balance because we're not aware of our own souls and the souls of our children.

We discover our own souls and the souls of our children more easily by keeping psychologically and spiritually balanced. We are more centered: upsetting incidents don't throw us off track as easily. We have a clearer picture of life because we can see many sides of an issue. We avoid focusing narrowly on one aspect of a person so our view is less distorted.

When Bonnie and I talk to parents about nurturing the souls of their children, we see their faces light up. "I'd forgotten about that," they tell us. They recognize that they haven't paid attention to this dimension of their children because they are concentrating on academic and/or athletic development.

I asked one couple to tell me the first thought that comes to their minds when they think of their twelve-year-old daughter. "She gets all

As," they proudly replied. They might just as well have been talking about their dog, "He's a great watchdog," or their computer, "It performs so well."

It was only when I asked them what made her different from everybody else that the parents began searching for their daughter's soul. They went on to describe how she sings in the shower, talks baby-talk to their seventy-pound German Shepherd, and nursed a sick sparrow back to health. They glowed with pride as they recalled how she'd comforted a friend who wasn't picked as a cheerleader, and then fumed when Mom and Dad grounded her for missing her curfew. They surprised themselves as they began to recognize all the personal qualities that make their daughter unique. Their balanced awareness uncovered her soul.

A father admitted he seemed to be in touch with the soul of his six-year-old son but not his thirteen-year-old daughter. He enjoyed playing with the boy, felt very warm toward him, seldom pressured him, and was patient with his son's mistakes. On the contrary, toward his teenage daughter the father was more demanding. He constantly registered his disappointments at her efforts, felt she was lazy, and jumped on her every mistake. Our talk on the soul caused him to reflect on the disparity in dealing with his children. He realized how connected he felt toward his son and how distant toward his daughter. Like many fathers of teenage girls, he was puzzled by her recent need to pull back from him a little. He felt rejected. He felt a sense of loss at her diminishing need for him. He realized he had been punishing her for developing normally. More than ever, she needed him to nurture her soul.

I suggested he start by trying to enjoy her as she is instead of micromanaging her life. Talk to her about what she feels is important instead of lecturing her. Ask her about her dreams instead of telling her about his plans for her. These are avenues to the souls of our children.

In the pressure to prepare our kids for our competitive, computerized world, we have lost sight of their souls and of our own psychological and spiritual balance. We are overloaded by contradictory information on how to raise our children: on diet, medical care, discipline, education, socializing, sibling rivalry, parenting, activities, TV, peers, and on and on. We spend our few free moments thinking up ways to make broccoli seem as appetizing as hot dogs, worrying about our kids' school performance, after-school activities, and how they're getting along with peers. We've come to see our kids as tasks to be done, responsibilities to be met. Ever diligent to chart their progress, we unleash an avalanche of questions when they come home from school or a Brownie meeting.

We hold our children up like an x-ray to so-called norms we find in parenting books. We feel successful if they "fit in" and are puzzled if they don't. More importantly, when our children don't fit in, we wonder where we have failed. We now spend so much time rating ourselves as parents that we forget to see our children as individuals. We are so absorbed in measuring their tangible success, we forget to ask "Who are they?" Inevitably, some new study or opinion comes to the rescue, like flash cards or playing Beethoven for infants. We eagerly turn to the new panacea in relief, seeking the missing ingredient to our obviously faulty recipe. We are becoming domestic engineers where our homes are factories. And our children have become products.

We are obsessed with measurement as a criterion for being a good parent. Percentiles, IQ, SAT scores, grades, and first place honors are the proofs, the measure of our success. When our own kids were in school sports, Bonnie and I used to watch parents taking down the "stats" of their children's performances: the number of tackles, passes caught in football, time differences in swimming. Mom and Dad were so preoccupied with measurements that they missed the simple joy of watching their child.

We don't hear parents describing their children as thoughtful, kind, friendly, honest — words that are close to the soul. One day I overheard a mom and a dad after a baseball game talking to their son. The boy had played wonderfully. They told him his "stats" were down from the last game, and that he had to make sure he would improve them next game. *The boy was in fifth grade!* The perplexed look on the little boy's face must have made him feel he didn't measure up to his parents' expectations despite having done so well.

Compare this to a set of parents who sounded balanced. It was after a junior varsity volleyball game that I listened to the father talking to his teenage daughter. Her team had just lost. The father put his arm around his daughter and asked, "Did you have a good time?" "Oh, it was so much fun," she answered. Her relaxed, easy posture, as she spoke, reflected the psychological balance of her dad and his connection to a deeper part of his daughter.

Whenever we talk to parents about nurturing the souls of their children, we usually ask for examples of when a parent felt he or she actually touched their child's soul. One father told us how his twelve-year-old boy was up to bat with his team one run behind in the final game of the league championship. There were two outs and the boy's team had the bases loaded. It was the last of the ninth. The father felt the tension in his own body; his hands were sweating, he found it difficult to breathe, praying that his boy would come through for his team. As the opposing pitcher threw the ball, the father was aware of the families of the players who were sitting on the edge of their seats. He said it felt like the final dramatic moment of a movie. His son had a chance to be a hero. The father heard the deep voice of the umpire as his son let the pitch sail past him. "Strike three! You're out!"

The father described how hard it was for him not to focus on the disappointed faces of his son's teammates and their parents. He had all he could do not to angrily ask his son why he'd let that last pitch go by. But when he saw the crestfallen look on his son's face and the tears in the boy's eyes, he knew his son needed his soul healed, not a judgmental lecture. Dad put his arm firmly around his son's shoulders instead, and shared how he himself had struck out in crucial games. "You did that too, Dad?" his boy asked. Watching hope light up in his son's eyes, the father felt their souls had connected.

Dreams

Clearly, we have to help develop our children's potential in as many areas as possible. The problem is that, as important as academics and performances are, they cannot be our exclusive concerns. If we focus only on measurement and achievement, we miss the souls of our children. We also miss their dreams.

Noreen, a pretty thirteen-year-old girl, was brought to me for counseling. She was an excellent student, a good athlete, and popular with her peers. She was also depressed. For the life of them, her parents could not figure out why. Yet it wasn't hard to find out. She talked to me in a monotone about her academic and athletic accomplishments. But when I asked her about her dreams, it was like I had switched on her high beams. She became animated and expressive as she spoke of wanting to become a famous actress. As if I had touched her soul with a magic wand, she blossomed on the spot. She told me she had never mentioned her dream to her parents because they would have dismissed it.

The point is not whether Noreen really has a chance to become a famous actress. The point is that she needs the dream. As parents, we shouldn't belittle, or make light of our children's dreams. *Their dreams are part of their souls.*

Noreen's situation seems to symbolize a growing problem we see with families, parents taking away their children's dreams too early, or substituting their own dreams in an effort to prepare them for the real world. We seem to have forgotten that *dreams warm our souls when we are young just as memories do when we are old.*

Touching Your Children's Souls

When we consciously explore the soul of our child, we enter a world of mystery, of unpredictability, of observation, of wonder, of focusing on understanding the child as profoundly as possible. Every child's soul is unique. There's no assembly line here; no "stats" to depend on. Instead, we enter a world of spirituality.

There is something sacred about the word "soul." I'm not using "sacred" in a religious sense, but in its meaning of being singularly worthy of respect. In this sense, "soul" encourages us to loosen control, to become ready to watch and learn. To understand the soul of another is to appreciate that person's deepest reality. Like the line from Victor Hugo's *Les Miserables,* "to love another person is to see the face of God."

Once we value our child's soul along with his academic achievement, athletic performance, or career potential, we take the first step toward greater intimacy. "Soul-searching" means recognizing that something singularly wonderful is happening here, right in front of us. It means realizing we participate as much by *watching* as by *directing.*

The chance to touch the soul of your child isn't something that happens every moment. Most of the time, we go from day to day dealing with the ordinary ups and downs of life — homework, laundry, cooking, schlepping the kids to school and doctors' appointments. However, there are those unanticipated moments when we have the chance to touch the souls of our children like when they come to us for help or want to share something. We need to be watchful so that when those special times do come, we won't miss them because we have our heads buried in our clipboards, jotting down the "stats."

You may not realize it, but you already know how it feels to touch the soul of your child. Remember the sense of wonder and mystery the first time you laid eyes on your child? You weren't comparing his IQ score to the baby in the next bassinet. You simply drank him in, soaking up his unique presence.

Recently Bonnie and I were on an airplane returning to Los Angeles from Phoenix, seated across the aisle from a young father who looked like he was in his early thirties. Throughout the entire hour-and-fifteen-minute flight, he was completely wrapped up with the tiny pink bundle in his arms, kissing her and talking to her. We could hear her infectious giggle and contented murmurs as her dad cooed and made funny faces, oblivious of the nearby passengers enjoying this tender scene. Father and daughter were touching each other's souls.

Sometimes we come closest to touching the souls of our children when they are sleeping. We don't have to scold or teach them at that moment. I remember how I used to sit on the side of my children's beds and just stare at their innocent beauty. It took my breath away.

Let one of your children fall sick, and you quickly connect to his soul. Deficiency notices, grades, achievements all vanish when you stand by the bed of your sick child. It took an incident with our daughter to bring this lesson home to us.

Kathleen was in the seventh grade at the time. She was staying at the home of her girlfriend's grandparents in Solvang, a quaint, picturesque town with a Danish atmosphere, surrounded by large ranches, about one-hundred-twenty miles north of our home in Los Angeles. We were at home when we got that dreaded phone call at about 8:00 p.m. telling us that our daughter needed emergency surgery to save her life. We will never forget that trip. We bundled our young son, Michael, in the back seat of the car and made the longest two-hour car trip of our lives. Neither Bonnie nor I spoke. Our thoughts were too frightening to share. What if she were to die? What if she were permanently injured? All the long-forgotten prayers of my priesthood flooded my memory as I tried to bargain with God for the life of our daughter. The fear of losing Kathleen connected us straight to her soul. She fully recovered, thank God. But even now, as I write these words, I relive the panic of that long night.

When you touch your child's soul, you learn to know her more deeply. A seven-year-old girl told Bonnie how frightened she was every time her parents screamed at each other. She would hide under her bed, trembling. The girl was always afraid that when she came out of her room after the screaming stopped, one of them would be gone. The parents were so engrossed in their own problems that they didn't recognize her terror.

Sadly, this is not an isolated case. In too many families, parents, when angered, feel justified in shouting profanities at each other in full view of their terrified children. When Bonnie and I point this out to parents, they frequently tell us they never realized how their own out-of-control behavior can affect their children. Children's souls remain undernourished and go underground when parents lose control.

In Touch with Your Own Soul

But there's another, more fundamental step in getting in touch with the soul of your child. *Get in touch with your own soul.* You have to bring your own life into a psychological and spiritual balance before you can appreciate your own soul. You have to value your own soul before you can appreciate your child's.

Take a moment now and think about your own behavior. Do you "lose it" in front of your kids? Do you and your partner scream at each other where the children can overhear you? Do you threaten divorce or to leave the family whenever you're angry? Take another moment and think about the effect your behavior has on your children. This is an essential step toward nurturing the souls of our children.

When Bonnie and I talk to parent groups on "Nurturing the Souls of Our Children," we usually begin with a relaxation exercise and a brief meditation. This helps the audience of stressed parents put their worries and concerns aside and, perhaps, get closer to their own souls. Each time we give this talk, some parents begin to tear. They often report they get in touch with their children's souls — perhaps for the first time since their children were infants. After one such session, a young mother tearfully shared with us how she had been so absorbed with her twelve-year-old son's studies and activities that she had not realized, until that very moment, that she'd been missing his soul. Several weeks later we met a father who had been at the talk. He told us that the idea of nurturing a child's soul had made an impact on the way he sees his own children. What pleased him most, he added, was that "I feel closer to them now. I enjoy them so much more. I'm noticing how much calmer our house is without me just concentrating on their academic performances and behavior. What surprised me most was that they seem more content. I kind of feel I've gotten in touch with my own soul."

Here are three ways we have found useful in helping parents to find their souls.

1. Slow Down

Our souls hide in the quiet, unhurried silences of life. Great religious leaders like Moses, Jesus, and Buddha knew the value of stopping to rest and reflect especially before momentous decisions. Moses spent forty days and forty nights on Mt. Sinai communing with God (Yahweh) before he came down with the two tablets on which were written the Ten Commandments. Jesus retreated to the Garden of Gethsemane before he faced his crucifixion. Buddha experienced the Great Enlightenment (the major teaching of Buddhism which revealed to him the way of salvation through suffering) while he was sitting meditating under a tree. Religious Orders are wise also. They provide a yearly retreat for their members where they unhurriedly search their souls reflecting on how they lived the past year and how they might do better next year.

We live in an ever-faster pace in a world that encourages us to buy cars that go from zero to sixty in record time, to buy a computer that can download at sixty-four billion bytes a second, to grasp the Network News and local and national political positions in fifteen-to-thirty-second sound-bytes, and to expect instantaneous relief from pain with quick-acting medication. We are not given the chance to slowly process upsetting news. Media anchors deftly slip from savage murders of innocent people to basketball scores in the same breath, leaving searing images in our minds like half-cooked food laying undigested in our stomachs. We don't even have time to consider the harmful effects of racing around like rats in a maze. In our determination to do more in less time, we've lost our psychological and spiritual balance.

I saw a sign in my neighborhood fast-food restaurant that said if you had to wait more than three minutes to be served, you would get your food free. It definitely impacted my own sense of balance. I found myself caught between hoping I *wouldn't* be served within the three-minute time limit — so I could get the order free — and hoping I *would* be served, because I was in a hurry. Standing in line waiting to place my order, I noticed the frenzied pace of the workers rushing their orders to the cooks and racing back with the filled ones, narrowly missing each other in the cramped space. I too got caught up in the drama. I spit out my order — *Number 3* (hamburger, fries and a drink) — and nodded like a general on inspection when the clerk barked it back in the same tempo. By the time I came out of the mini-madness with my overcooked hamburger and half-frozen bun, hastily thrown together in two minutes and fifty-five seconds —I checked — my hands were sweating and my heart was racing. This was not food for my soul. Given the state my stomach was in, it didn't do my body much good, either.

Once I got over the indigestion, I had a good, long, soul-searching talk with myself about the rat-race symptoms so common to all of us today. Now, when I stand in a long line at a bank, I turn the wait into a chance to slow down. I look around at the decor, try to guess the life story of my "fellow-liners," and marvel at their wasted anger, anger I used to share.

"Why don't they have more tellers?" mutters a small, thin, stylishly-dressed woman of about fifty. I notice she keeps glancing at her watch. I decide she's on her lunch hour.

"This is the last time I'm doing business at this bank," a young man behind me says in a loud, threatening tone. He's casually dressed in jeans, a tank top and sandals. Definitely not an office type. I remember him from last week saying the identical words. By the time I'm next, most of the eight or ten people in line have added their disgruntled voices to the choir of complaint. So much wasted energy and bile churning up their souls needlessly, I decide. I feel like giving them a mini-sermon on the spot. But aside from a serene-looking young woman of about twenty who appears unaffected by the scene, this congregation doesn't look receptive to my ideas. I just hope they aren't headed for the freeway — we have enough road rage out there already.

Another good place to slow down is the local supermarket. You can even catch up on the current celebrity gossip. If I'm not in a hurry, I select the longest check-out line. This gives me time to read the latest tabloids, which, of course, I would never stoop so low as to actually buy.

A favorite "slow down" time for Bonnie is when she orders a drink at the drive-through window of a fast-food restaurant. She finds a brief respite from her busy schedule as she waits in line to give her order. She never minds how many cars there are ahead of her. She listens to soothing music and waits contentedly for her turn to be served. She feels it's one of the few places mothers can hide from the constant demands of their family.

You might look through your day to discover where you could accept waiting as a chance to relax. Maybe the car line at school, or on hold on the telephone waiting to talk to a real person. All of us can probably find some moments where we can take advantage of the wait instead of complaining about it.

2. Accept Your Limitations

Marie, a young mother of three small children, told Bonnie she did not know how to say "no" to the pleas for help she got from her family, her work, her friends, her church, her neighbors, and her children's school. Her husband was the primary supporter of the family, but she worked part-time. She also did all the shopping, cooking and most of their children's caretaking. In addition, she was room mom for two of her children's classrooms and was in charge of a school fund drive. She was team mother for her son's soccer team. She taught Sunday School. Recently she'd been made block captain for her Neighborhood Watch. What made her decide to see Bonnie was a recent request from her pastor. He'd asked her to organize a family life program. When she started to tell him she was already overwhelmed, he cut her short saying, "I know you can do it. We really need you." She agreed to his request. Then she hung up the phone and started to cry. She realized she had a "problem" when she couldn't stop. She wasn't aware of how next to impossible it was for her to say "no." Her sobbing caught her by surprise. She was out of balance and didn't even know it — out of touch with her soul.

Many women are like Marie. They view their individual identities within the context of their relationships. They need to be the center of their relationships. Like the web of a spider, they spin an interconnected set of threads anchored to themselves at the center. They attune themselves to the voices and needs of the people who make up the threads of their webs.

Society has fashioned this exaggerated role for women. Walk into any greeting card store on Mother's Day. The sentiment is usually gratitude from husbands and children who praise women for their one-hundred-percent availability to the needs of others. It's hard for women facing such social expectations to be in touch with their own souls. Bonnie tells women that being one-hundred-percent selfless is neurotic. In her *Women's Journey* groups, she points out that women become better caretakers by including themselves in their caretaking. In fact, Research Psychologist Carol Gilligan found that women who take care of themselves in addition to caring for others demonstrate a higher level of moral development.

Viewed in this context, it wasn't surprising that Marie had lost touch with her soul. She couldn't tell the difference between self-protective and selfish. All she could hear were the voices of others: her children, her husband, her kids' school, her neighbors, her boss, and finally, the proverbial straw that broke the camel's back, her pastor. When she couldn't stop the tears, she was forced to pay attention to something deep within her. Her soul was crying out for balance.

Bonnie, who also finds it hard to say "no," shared with Marie what she does when facing a request for help. "That sounds like a good idea," she'll say to the requester. "Let me check my schedule and I'll get back to you." This gives her time to reign in her automatic tendency to say "yes." With more time — and a little distance — she can find a way to politely get out from under when she's reached her limit.

Bonnie helped Marie see that resentment and even depression are often the results of not being able to say "no." Marie admitted she began to feel angry at everyone making unreasonable demands on her, and that, helpless to assert herself, she was slipping into depression. Slowly, she began to understand that her family, friends, and even the pastor would not be devastated if she politely and firmly declined a request for help when her instincts signaled she had reached her limit. An interesting aside is that Marie went back to the pastor, this time simply and clearly saying she would not be able to be on the committee. "It worked like magic," she told Bonnie. "He said, 'Okay, I'll get somebody else.' " Marie began to understand this process and was soon working herself back into balance, coming closer to nurturing her soul.

3. A Sense of Humor

Humor is a bridge that connects us to our souls. One sizzling summer day, Bonnie went to the local bicycle shop to meet our college-age daughter, Kathleen. It was in an area where Bonnie often ran into some of her clients so she was particularly aware of her professional image. Waiting outside the shop, my navy-suited wife spotted two young people in bright red lifeguard suits weaving their way across the burning asphalt of the parking lot. They attracted quite a crowd as they half-stumbled, laughing uproariously, the barefoot girl riding the young man piggyback. This pair, Bonnie thought, could stand a few lessons in decorum. Only, as the pair neared her, those hilarious screams started to sound all too familiar. Then she felt a sudden wave of panic.

Oh, my God! Could it be? she said to herself. It was. The two young lifeguards were our then nineteen-year-old son Michael and his twenty-one-year-old sister Kathleen. At that moment, Bonnie realized she had to choose: lecture them about the danger of piggybacking through a crowded parking lot of moving cars (a little late at their ages!), inquire as to the whereabouts of Kathleen's shoes, remind them of her professional image, or simply watch and enjoy the fun they were having.

Seeing the joy lighting up their eyes, Bonnie made the last choice. And she felt herself connect to their souls. By choosing to share their joy, she strengthened the spiritual balance of all three of them. She nurtured her soul as well as theirs.

Try to consciously keep the idea of nurturing your children's souls for two weeks. If you can do this — and I warn you now, it's not easy — you'll begin to distinguish the difference between little things and important things. You'll start to focus on your children's zest for life rather than on the stereo that's too loud. You'll find yourself delighting in their overall good health rather than the spilled glass of milk or messy room.

Eight Tips to Nurture the Soul of Your Child

1. Put measurements on the back burner.

Pick one day each month (like the first or the fifteenth) to *not* concentrate on your children's report cards, academic placements, appropriate weight and height and any other numbers that describe them.

2. Focus on who your children are.

With the measurements and numbers put aside, ask yourself *Who is my child?* This is a tough question because the answer has to come from within yourself. You can't turn to a chart or a statistical profile to help you. Don't be in a hurry to answer the question. You may have to wait for the answer to come from your own attitudes and feelings about your child. Don't be surprised if you feel a few tears roll down your cheeks. It's a sign you're getting closer to his soul.

3. Listen to what your children say.

Try this. When your child is talking, don't say a word. Just listen. It doesn't matter if she is complaining, criticizing, crying, laughing, or even complimenting you. (Don't bet on that last one, though.) Just be quiet. Pay attention to her tone, her emphasis on certain words, the intensity in her voice, or maybe the confusion she shows. Listening can help you to understand life from her point of view. Sometimes even very young children can answer a common question with wisdom. At one of our talks, a father told of the answer his four-year-old daughter gave to an adult who asked her how old she was. In a very serious tone, she replied, "I'm four now, but I'm practicing to be five."

4. Watch them while they sleep.

This is easier when they are young. Just stand or sit quietly beside your child's bed. Watch his face. Most young children tend to sleep deeply and peacefully. But sometimes a child will be dreaming and you'll see him smile or frown — depending upon the dream. Pay attention to his breathing, the position of his body, and how he moves in his sleep. These quasi-meditative moments can bring you a sense of tranquility.

5. Drink them in with your eyes.

Concentrate on looking at your child. Watch her eyes, her face, her gestures, especially the movement of her hands. This last is a valuable clue to her true feelings — in spite of what she says. You may learn things about her that you never knew before.

6. Let all your senses be attuned to them.

Let your hand rest on his head or arm while you are close. Touching your child in a loving way brings a protective intimacy, comforts your child, and nurtures your own soul. No words need to be spoken to communicate your feelings to your child. I try not to miss the chance to briefly put my hand on my children's shoulders or arms. I give them a quick kiss on the top of their heads if I walk by and they are studying or reading. In addition to sight and sound, even our sense of smell can connect us to our children. Of course, with a teenage boy at least, you might want to wait until after he's showered.

7. Enjoy them.

Occasionally, back off from just feeling responsible for your children. Step away for a moment from needing to advise, guide, teach, discipline, direct, shape, monitor, check, and all the other supervisory ways through which we parent them. These duties are, of course, part of the very essence of parenting. But every now and then just try to enjoy your kids. Watch them having fun with their friends, laughing at their favorite TV shows. Listen to them singing in the shower or lip-synching the latest CD — that is, if they turn down the volume.

8. Laugh with them.

Children have their own kind of humor. We have to develop a taste for it much like they have to develop a taste for broccoli. Kids' humor is exaggerated, silly, slightly gross, spontaneous, and almost always just plain "off the wall." We miss a great chance for a close connection with our children if we don't make an effort to enjoy their humor. Bonnie tells parents even if they don't understand what their children are laughing at (not an uncommon experience) to at least enjoy their laughter.

As you do these things for even two weeks, you'll find that you're beginning to touch and nurture their souls, and in the process, you just may rediscover your own.

Getting in touch with one's soul is a life-long process. A nurse friend of ours found the following words written by her mother shortly before her mother's death. They show a woman who was in touch with her soul.

I hear my soul voice and much of the time I enjoy sitting with it, dreaming with it, sharing it with others. The barriers of time and the human heart hold me back, keep me quiet. I want to write and travel. I want to feel the ocean spray, walk in gardens, play with children, write about what has been wonderful about life. I want to visit old friends and be warmed by their love

Our friend's mother didn't put a period at the end of the last sentence, which her daughter found significant. The soul, after all, has no ending.

CHAPTER IV

Affluenza: Are We Giving Our Children Too Much?

In my dealing with my child, my Latin and Greek, my accomplishments and my money stead me nothing; but as much soul as I have avails.

Ralph Waldo Emerson

About seventy-five parents were already gathered in the spacious home when Bonnie and I arrived for our talk. The host couple and a small committee of parents had prepared a lovely variety of elegant desserts and beverages. Two comfortable chairs had been set out for us behind a large, ornate coffee table. Across from us, ten rows of well-dressed parents sat on folding, white chairs. Behind us, large bay windows ran from parqueted floor to cathedral ceiling, displaying an evening panoramic view of the West San Fernando Valley, where the stars looked like diamonds on black velvet.

Most of the parents in this audience had children ranging from infants to early teenagers. They'd put a lot of time and energy juggling homework, bedtime, dinner, and baby-sitters in order to free up two hours that evening to learn about parenting.

The topic of our talk was *Are We Giving Our Children Too Much?* It was a timely topic for these upwardly-mobile, financially-successful parents who were beginning to see a downside to providing so much for their children. It was precisely for this kind of parent that Wealth researcher Frederick Croker Whitman coined the word *affluenza*. The word describes a growing phenomenon in today's children — the expectation of an affluent lifestyle without the corresponding ambition and self-confidence that would allow them to finance it on their own. More and more we hear about ungrateful kids who expect everything to be handed to them. The questions we were addressing that night were: Are we giving our children so many material things that they are becoming too self-indulgent? Are we doing so much for them that they are becoming ungrateful? Are they becoming psychologically and spiritually unbalanced?

Each time we talk on this topic, we show a cartoon of a rabbit-like family drawn by Matt Groening. The rabbit parents are sitting on a sofa; there are mounds of wrapped packages under the Christmas tree. A little preteen rabbit stands by the doorway with this caption over his head, "This better be good."

Giving and doing too much for them doesn't seem to make them happier. Researchers tell us that the average income of Americans has doubled since the 1950s. We have twice as many cars and eat out twice as often. We have more air conditioning, CD sound systems, and color

TVs. However, the proportion of "very happy" people has decreased from 35 percent to 30 percent. At the same time, the divorce rate has doubled, teenage suicide tripled, juvenile crime shot up fivefold, and diagnoses of clinical depression have increased. Looking at our country's materialistic culture, we have to conclude that economic growth apparently does not increase human morale.* As parents we have to actively prevent our materialistic culture from throwing our families off balance. Excessive materialism does not nurture a child's soul.

It takes a healthy family to keep balanced psychologically and spiritually. Affluenza chokes out the spiritual side of our kids' psychological development. Unfortunately, we can't always protect them from the constant bombardment of instant gratification that comes from movies, TV, magazines and billboards. The best way we can immunize our children from this "sickness" is to develop a healthy balance between our own material and spiritual values and to pass these on to our children.

At a talk we gave in San Francisco, a young, affluent couple described how their eight-year-old son opened a Hanukkah present his grandparents had given him. Throwing it across the floor, he screamed, "I don't want this!"

The parents were momentarily paralyzed. On the one hand, they were angry at his inappropriate behavior. On the other hand, they feared that stifling his feeling would harm him psychologically. While we encourage our children to express their feelings, we have to teach them that others have feelings too. This would have been a good time for the parents to take their son aside and explain that the proper behavior would be to thank his grandparents for their thoughtfulness. Later on, he could tell his parents that he didn't like the gift.

At another talk, a single mother, who struggles to make ends meet as a cleaning lady, complained that her six-year-old daughter and four-year-old son never appreciate all the toys and games she gives them in spite of the fact she works overtime to buy those things. She doesn't want her children to experience the deprivation she knew: second-hand clothes from a thrift shop, Christmas and birthdays with few (if any) gifts and scarcely enough to eat — never mind about toys. She wants her children to enjoy all the good things she never had. She realized that she had lost her own balance in concentrating on giving her children material objects without teaching them the other values of self-discipline, delay of gratification and a sense of gratitude.

Bonnie and I witnessed our own children lose their balance in the face of gifts. I recall one Christmas morning when our children were about five and seven. Bonnie and I had spent the night wrapping their presents and tucking them under the tree. We were feeling warm and excited anticipating their sweet faces as they joyfully opened up each gift. Instead, our son and daughter began to fight as soon as they woke up, arguing over who should open the gifts first. As much as we hated to do it, we sent them back to their rooms on Christmas morning. After a few minutes, which seemed like an eternity to the children, we called them back. The rest of the day was wonderful.

Demand Lists vs Wish Lists

Remember how gift-giving on special days like birthdays, Christmas and Hanukkah used to be fun? Children made out "wish lists," hoping to receive just a few of the items. Today, wish lists have become "demand lists." To avoid disappointing — or even angering — their children, parents nowadays often feel obligated to buy them all of the items, sometimes even going into debt to do so.

We encourage you to return to the wish list. Don't expect your children to be happy with this change. They won't be, at first. Give them a month's advance notice; children do better when they know what's coming. Good teachers have always known this. Visit a classroom where the children are learning a lot and are calm. You'll see how the students know exactly what the teacher expects and when she expects it. Like a teacher, you have to be clear and firm. Don't give your kids the idea that you feel bad or guilty about the new system. They'll grumble. They're kids. Bet on it. But, whatever you do, don't lecture or expect them to understand the reasoning behind your new approach. A father, who tried this approach, told me he explained to his children that they would thank him for doing this when they were grown-ups. I would have loved to see the look on their faces. Parental lectures often end up with us frustrated and our kids confused.

Bonnie and I have learned through experience that the most effective method is to simply announce that the demand list isn't working, and that our family is going back to the wish list. By saying "our family," you're teaching your kids that this is part of your family values. When your kids object — and they most certainly will — lamenting that their friends always get what they want, don't put the other families down. Simply say, "Well, that's how their families work. But in our family we do it differently."

One couple, who took our advice and braved the wrath of their children by establishing the wish list, reported that for the first time in several years they actually had fun buying and wrapping the packages. They felt like parents again rather than UPS delivery persons.

Surprises

Children need to be surprised. In our family we have the custom of filling the children's Christmas stockings with small surprises, inexpensive gifts that are amusing and fit each child's personality. Bonnie and I have great fun looking for these gifts. Our children enjoy the small surprises. If your child has no idea of the contents of a box, the element of surprise increases the enjoyment. The anticipation and the process of removing the ribbon and wrapping paper add to the sense of mystery. There is magic in opening a gift box and finding a surprise. If you allow your children to make a demand list, you take away an important part of their childhood.

Whether your children receive everything without working for it or whether they get nothing no matter how hard they try, they develop the same problem. Both groups can become depressed. Since their personal effort is meaningless, they feel helpless to influence their own destiny. In our therapy practice, parents will bring a child in and say, "She's a problem at school and is always sad. We don't know why. We've always given her everything she ever wanted." We suggest that could be the problem. She seldom feels the joy that comes from accomplishing something on her own.

At the other end of the economic scale, I recall the sense of despair and hopelessness I saw in the faces of starving children in Peru.

Nothing they did alleviated their hunger. Eventually, they even stopped begging. One small boy had so given up that when I offered him a few coins, I had to take his hand and press the money into it. His short life-time of futile efforts left him emotionally paralyzed. I still wonder what eventually became of him. When I returned to the same place a few months later, he was not there. Personal effort without a hope of success can kill the soul.

Whether we give children too much or not enough, if their own input is meaningless, they may feel unprepared to control their own destiny.

A Child's Two Cents Worth

Children seem to feel better by putting in their own two cents worth. Too many parents, without realizing it, may lower their children's self-worth by overloading them with material things. Some parents make things even worse by doing for their children what they can do for themselves. A good example of this is a school science fair. Visit one. What do you see? Elaborate, sophisticated projects bearing the students' names, but the glow of proud accomplishment lights up the faces of their parents.

Bonnie met Bill, the father of twelve-year-old Kathy, racing to the library to do research for his daughter's California Mission project while she was at soccer practice. With the best of intentions, Bill was doing something for his daughter that she needed to do for herself. Bill will become resentful. Kathy — who'll start feeling she can never measure up to her father's work — will expect Dad to rescue her. This is a recipe for a resentful father and an ungrateful daughter. It can throw both father and daughter off balance, and nurturing the soul is unlikely.

Like many parents, Bill didn't want his daughter to miss anything and so, overscheduled her. We are not saying parents should not involve themselves in their children's projects. We are referring to parents who, after overprogramming their children, have to rescue them and, perhaps, undermine their self-worth.

Gratitude

Parents often ask us what they can do about their ungrateful children. They tell us the more they give and the more they do for their children, the less grateful their kids are.

Gratitude is an awareness of another's effort to help us, the ability to step out of ourselves and recognize someone else's efforts on our behalf. Children tend to be self-absorbed and narcissistic. They are fragile and need most of their energy to form their own sense of self. They have to be taught how to be grateful. For most children it doesn't come naturally. Excessive giving can increase a child's self-absorption and sense of entitlement to the point that all he can see is the gift and not the giver.

We believe having children write thank-you notes for gifts at birthdays and holidays helps them become aware of gratitude. If children are old enough to write, they should write the notes in their own words. Younger ones can help mom or dad compose the note. Having your children say "thanks" to service people or those who might do a kindness (like holding a door open) reinforces the custom of expressing gratitude. Of course, the best lesson for children is to witness their parents showing gratitude to others.

Economy Class

When our son Michael was twelve, he wanted to buy a pair of pump basketball shoes. He believed the shoes would help him jump higher, as was suggested by the advertisement. We spoke to our son's coach, who said a good pair of shoes cost about $75. The pump shoes went for $120. We told Michael we would pay for the reasonable shoes. If he wanted the more expensive kind, he would have to use money from his savings. We would pay for "economy class." Naturally, he wasn't too thrilled by our line of thinking. However, he decided slam-dunking was worth the money. Recently, our now worldly-wise son of twenty-one recalled this incident almost in our own words. "Boy," he told us laughing, "was that a dumb thing to do, waste my money like that." Having learned a lesson or two about dumb decisions ourselves, Bonnie and I just nodded to each other.

Delay of Gratification

Another way you can help your kids avoid the affluenza bug is to teach them to wait for some of the things they want "immediately, if not before." Remember how parents used to talk about strengthening a child's character? When I was a child, we were expected to give up something we liked for Lent, the forty-day period before Easter Sunday. Besides the spiritual benefits, your character was certainly put to the test — especially if you decided to give up candy. Now character is reserved for the off-beat and unpredictable.

But strength of character early in life can pay great dividends later on. Psychologist Walter Mischel of Stanford found out that the ability to delay gratification can have a long-term payoff. He tracked four-and-a-half-year-olds into middle and late adolescence. He found out that the toddlers who were able to wait for a treat later as adolescents showed some valuable qualities. From preschool age to adolescence, the parents of these kids consistently guided them away from instant gratification. They were willing to resist disappointing their children by not giving in to all their children's demands. By the time the toddlers reached their teens, they had high standards, were attentive, showed good concentration, expressed ideas well, and were able to cope maturely with stress. They also did as well socially as they did intellectually. In other words, they were better equipped to deal with whatever life threw at them.

The ability to postpone instant gratification gives our children the best shot at keeping their psychological and spiritual balance when they hit those potentially-destructive choices like premature sex, drugs and alcohol. Unfortunately, the opportunity to engage in such things is rampant today. Ask any middle- or high-school child from a public or private school, and he or she will tell how easy it is to buy drugs on campus. The surest way we guide our children through this labyrinth of self-destructive choices is by giving them a sense of self-worth and staying emotionally close to them — nurturing their souls. The "high" that children get from being intimately connected to their parents is far more pleasurable and lasting than any drug.

Permissive and indulgent parents who give their kids whatever they ask for may bring a smile to the child's face for the moment, but at what future cost? Bonnie and I worry about the future of the little tykes we see in toy stores and supermarkets who demand — and get! — whatever first captures their attention.

FHB

Even children can learn that the needs of others sometimes come first. As a child, there were times when my parents had to struggle just to put food on the table. And in our large Irish family, there was no predicting how many "relatives" might show up for supper. Many were the times when an aunt, uncle, cousin, or neighbor just "happened" to drop by at suppertime. Many more were the times when *all* of them stopped by. Whenever the drop-in guests outnumbered the amount of food, my mother would casually mention "FHB." My three sisters, my brother and I knew the code: *Family Hold Back* meant we were to trim our appetites. We learned that good hosts take care of their guests first — not a bad awareness for children to develop.

Say "No"

We encourage you to say "no" to children more often. Some parents find this difficult to do. The smile on our children's faces has become the principal barometer to measure how much we care for them. If your child is pleased, you feel like a good parent. If your child frowns, you feel you've failed. However, putting your parental worth in the hands of your child is a serious mistake for both of you. Your kids won't be able to decide what kind of parent you've been until they have kids of their own. Then that secret wish of every parent — *I hope you have a kid just like you* — may come true.

Failing to say "no" at appropriate times can backfire on you and your child. I noticed a father in the supermarket pushing his daughter of about four or five in the shopping cart. She kept asking him to hold different items. It became a game. He would give her an item and she would give it back to him, then ask for another one. Apparently our wives had given us similar shopping lists because we kept meeting on different aisles, searching for things like *balsamic vinaigrette* and *cumin.* Each time we passed I could see the father becoming more annoyed. Yet instead of simply stopping the game, he kept asking her when she would get tired of it. I felt like answering for her: "NEVER — she's a kid."

The next time we passed on the candy aisle, the little girl handed her father a box of cookies. He threw it back on the shelf, then screamed, "Can't you see I'm tired of this?! Why are you so selfish?" I watched the little girl's face go from delight to confusion and tears. What had been such a wonderful game with her dad abruptly turned into his getting angry, and she didn't have a clue why.

The father expected the four-year-old to be able to judge what would annoy an adult. It would have been better for him to call a halt when he no longer wanted to participate. His daughter would have been disappointed, true, but not confused. Instead, she was left with no idea of what she had done wrong. Her young mind couldn't make the leap from *Daddy laughing* to *Daddy yelling* without any warning.

Little children's minds are not sophisticated enough to figure out why we overreact. We have to interpret our emotions for them, saying something like, "Honey, Daddy's tired. I want you to sit in the cart while I look for the things on Mommy's list. Later we'll play this game again."

In the meantime our youngsters will inevitably reach the point where we disappoint them. Here we must be wise and understand that their criticism is a necessary step in the process of their separating from us. We have to keep our balance or we'll lose contact with their souls. As a seventeen-year-old know-it-all, fresh from my high school Sociology class, I remember lecturing my father on the social inequities of that time and the failure of his generation to find solutions. He listened patiently and simply said, "Well, maybe you'll be able to straighten out the world better than our generation has." His answer acknowledged that my criticism had some validity, but he wisely made me aware that I too would be held responsible some day. He resisted my attempt to paint his generation as complete failures.

When Bonnie was a high-school sophomore, she would feel compelled, at times, to lecture her family about the earth-shaking new facts she learned in school that day — as only an omniscient teenager can. Her father, who had a good sense of humor, patiently waited for his daughter to finish. Then he would say, solemnly, "The Queen has spoken." His humor allowed her to pontificate while keeping the family in balance.

Children think concretely. They live in a world of absolutes — wrong or right, good or bad. Compromise is difficult for them. We have to interpret for them. The eight-year-old boy who didn't get invited to the party is sure everyone hates him. The eleven-year-old girl who didn't make her school soccer team feels the coach hates her. When a parent screams at a child for misbehaving, the child will conclude not only that what he did was bad but that he is bad, too, unless the parent explains the difference. Adults come to see us in therapy convinced that they are defective or bad because of the demeaning things their parents continually said to them. The consequences of our unexplained, abrupt anger at our own children can cause them to lose confidence in themselves and to find difficulty in trusting others.

Setting Limits

Pleasing our children is only one dimension of parenting. Another, equally important, is setting appropriate limits. Often this is difficult, because they don't like it when we say "no." And they don't like us for saying it. So if we look to them for approval, setting limits is not the way to go. However, setting limits is essential in guiding our children wisely. We see the long view of life; our children don't. They simply haven't lived long enough. A recent case brought this home to me.

Maureen was not quite fifteen. At a party, she caught the eye of a twenty-one-year-old college student. When he asked her for a date, she was ecstatic. However, her parents refused to let her go. She was crushed, angry and humiliated. While she tried to glare them down with her *if-looks-could-kill* stare, they explained that she was too young to go on a single date, much less with a twenty-one-year-old man. They listened to her impassioned pleas that he was just short of angelic. They said "no" again. They held firm. Maureen's parents knew that she was not yet equipped to handle the subtle (and not-so-subtle) pressures that come with single dating. Her parents also were aware she would not understand their position until she became an adult.

Wants vs Needs

We need to resist our children when they confuse "want" with "need." Children may not know the difference. That's why they're so intense about asking for things, because they think that anything they want is a life-or-death *need*. Our job as parents is to teach them the difference. We recommend providing *all* of their needs but only *some* of their wants. Your child's disappointment at not getting what she wants is just as important in her journey to adulthood as the joy of getting it. The mix of disappointment and pleasure balance each other. Though Sigmund Freud and Mark Twain are not usually linked together, they both agreed that we can't experience pleasure if we've never known pain. We are doing an injustice to our kids if we don't teach them this lesson. Children who have been shielded from normal setbacks and disappointments can have a distorted view of life that can affect jobs and relationships in adulthood.

An increasing number of young people entering the job market don't want to have a boss. They want complete independence and a high salary immediately. Young couples start off their life together going into debt because they have to stock their wardrobe with designer clothes and their home with elegant furnishings. They have not yet learned to distinguish between wants and needs.

Our parents' generation and ours were raised expecting that struggle would be part of life. For example, my parents could not afford to buy me a bicycle. Each week I saved as much as I could from what I had earned delivering groceries. As I watched the money grow, I let myself feast on the anticipation of owning that bicycle. Each week the thrill got a little stronger. What I most remember about finally saving enough money to buy the bike is not the bicycle itself, but the thrill of plunking down the sixty dollars I'd earned.

Getting our kids to save for something is a lot tougher than before. Our children are used to seeing us put a card in an ATM and — like magic — money pops out. We pull out a credit card and walk away with whatever we want to buy. Children are used to getting what they want, fast. Today, kids not only want to see a new movie right away, but to see the first show the first day it comes out.

Advertising plays upon this tendency. Kids are "fair game" for marketing. You only have to watch a half-hour of TV on a Saturday morning to see how effectively advertising blurs the distinction between *want* and *need*. The goal of every commercial is to create a *need* for the food, drink, clothes, toys or game they advertise. And it works. It was one of these ads that convinced my twelve-year-old son he *needed* pump shoes. Trouble is, the ads are primarily designed to work for their sponsors' bottom lines. Those ads increase corporate profits, but ignore the long-term, possible destructive effects they may have on these future adults. I have never seen a commercial encouraging children to save up their money to buy a big ticket item like a bike. Delay of gratification is an unwelcome concept in advertising.

Dubium Juris vs Dubium Facti

In theology I learned the difference between *dubium juris* and *dubium facti*. These Latin phrases mean *a doubt of law* and *a doubt of reality*, respectively. An example of *dubium juris* would be coming to a traffic light on a lonely road, late at night with no other car in sight — not a place to linger. You have a choice to sit there until the light changes or drive right through the red light. The second choice breaks the law, but doesn't harm anyone.

An example of a *dubium facti*, on the other hand, is a hunter who sees what looks like a deer in the distance. He's almost sure it's a deer. *Almost.* But somewhere in the back of his mind he knows it could be something else, even a fellow hunter. He shoots anyway, on the chance that his first impression is right. According to the philosopher St. Thomas Aquinas, the hunter is guilty of killing a human being *even if he bags a deer.* He has a right to hunt, certainly. But, his conscience should remind him that his personal rights are not greater than his obligation to prevent harm to another.

In an environment where the rights of the individual are automatically trumpeted above the rights of others, it's easy to lose our psychological and spiritual balance. "Every man for himself" leads to chaos. Nurturing the soul of another demands that we are respectful not only of the other's rights, but also of his needs. Nurturing the soul of another means that we realize our actions always have an effect upon others. As parents, we can hardly nurture the souls of our children if we are callused toward others outside the home.

The Church has a concept that I now see is very wise. It is called "The Mystical Body." It means that the entire human race is considered one body. No matter how different the functions are, like the hand from the heart, or the distance between them like the ear from the foot, they are all vitally connected and have to work in harmony for the good of the whole to remain healthy. How wonderful it would be if this concept were understood by the world's different nations, ethnic groups and races.

Our job as parents would be easier if society were to keep a three-way balance between profits, First Amendment rights and the vulnerability of our children. It would be easier too, if society learned the difference between *dubium juris* and *dubium facti*. We've put the spotted owl on the endangered species list, yet we fail to recognize that we may be endangering the future of our children by allowing the entertainment and commercial industries to target them as a potential market. And for that, we *all* suffer the consequences.

Kids Pressuring Parents

Ever hear remarks like these?

"I *have* to have that designer jacket! Every one of my friends has one. I'll be the only kid without one."

"Why can't you be like all my friends' parents?"

"You're the strictest parents in the school. Why are you so stingy?"

If you have a good reason not to buy an item, *don't cave in.* We were giving a talk about affluenza in a private home not so long ago. One mother told us that her thirteen-year-old son overheard our ideas about giving and doing too much for our children. "Don't listen to them," he told her. "I don't want to have to start cleaning my bedroom."

She told us that she had been both giving and doing too much for her son and his two younger sisters. A couple of months later, we ran into the same mother at a local shopping center. She and her husband had taken our advice to heart, she said. With the kids cooperating more the house was calmer, she was less resentful, and even her thirteen-year-old cleaned his room with only minor complaints.

Our Weak Points

Our children know our weak points. Remember, they've been studying us since birth. Bonnie and I were giving a talk to parents at a National Convention in San Diego, California. One father, a married priest, related that whenever he put reasonable limits on the things his children wanted, they hit him with, "Yeah, sure, you were a priest. Now we have to suffer because you took a vow of poverty."

The father felt very guilty. Bonnie told him his background as a priest had nothing to do with the issue. The kids just knew what button to push. Had he not been a priest, they would have found something else to use, like him being from a different generation, or because he was the strictest parent in the neighborhood, or he didn't love them because they were the only kids who didn't have a video-gaming system, or . . . You've got a line or two to fill in yourself, I'm sure.

Children go for the emotional jugular. When our daughter was 10, we gave her a firm "no" about going to the mall unchaperoned. She was quiet for a moment. Then with her jaw jutting out and eyes flashing, she said, "I'm going over to your office and stand outside your door and tell your clients how mean you really are!" For the next few days, we found ourselves looking out the office window, half-expecting to see her with a protest sign.

Actions speak louder than words. It's a cliché we should live by. Children become stronger by watching us act appropriately. Holding our ground in the face of their "target practice" on us, we show them how to resist inappropriate pressure. Later, when they are pressured to experiment with premature sex, drugs and excessive drinking, they have our example to fall back on. Remember that study of preschoolers who could delay gratification and later became well-adjusted teenagers? In a nutshell, those kids just learned the word "no" young.

Sometimes saying "no" to our children is more loving than saying "yes." Some of the children Bonnie and I see are from homes where parents have lost their psychological and spiritual balance — where parents have not nurtured the souls of their children.

Joanne, for example, spent one Saturday morning cutting out designs for her eleven-year-old daughter Casey's science project. The girl herself spent the morning practicing the piano. Joanne sensed something was off since she finished fifth grade years ago. Yet here she was becoming her daughter's academic alter ego. Joanne told me she became aware that something was out of balance when she recognized her own resentment about the project. "I could understand how Casey might be miffed about doing the work," she told me, "But me? It wasn't even my project."

It would be better for Casey, she realized, if the girl did a simpler project, but did it by herself. Casey would probably get a better grade if her mom did most of the work, but it wouldn't do much for the girl's self-worth, not to mention her sense of honesty. Without the resentment Joanne was feeling — and by accepting her daughter's own work — mom would be in a much better balance to nurture her child's soul.

We can give our children too much by overloading them with too many activities. Then we have to rescue them from the overload we ourselves caused! While I was waiting for my turn to speak at a conference, I overheard a mother telling her friend how she had been preparing her children's lunches for twenty-three years. Her youngest, a thirteen-year-old daughter, was a member of the swim team, the water-polo team, a cheerleader, and a team leader of their church's teen program. She rattled off these activities with an obvious pride in a voice that sounded exhausted. What I *heard* was an overloaded mother with an overextended daughter, both precariously close to losing their balance. *And she wasn't even aware of it!*

I fantasized about finding a phone booth and stripping off my clothes to reveal a superman-like outfit with the words *Super-Balancer* emblazoned across the chest. I imagined leaping out before her and saying, "Excuse me, Ma'am, but you and your daughter are in grave danger of losing your balance. Let me save you from this emotional quicksand." Fortunately, my name was announced as the next speaker before I could get my shirt off.

Overprotective Parents

The world is not always a friendly place. Our children need to learn how to deal with setbacks while they still have us to fall back on. Sometimes we try to protect our children's feelings too much. Bonnie tells the story of a mother whose third grade daughter was not invited to a classmate's birthday party. To protect her from having her feelings hurt, the child's mother called the mother of another classmate (whose daughter *had* been invited) and asked her to get the girl invited.

In another case, Jim and Martha, devoted parents, bought their eight-year-old son Sean a trophy when he failed to win one at his school Sports Night. We cannot and should not protect our children from every unpleasant incident, even though we feel their pain.

We help them more by guiding them through the process of hurts and disappointments than by artificially protecting them. The third grade girl needed her mom to guide her through hurt feelings. Sean needed his parents' understanding, not a fake trophy.

Allowances vs Chores

Are we giving our children too much? brings up the questions of allowances and chores. Should children be given an allowance? At what age? How much? What about household chores? Should kids get paid for them? Should their allowance be withheld if they don't finish their chores? We try to answer these questions that often puzzle and confuse parents.

Through the years, Bonnie and I have seen parents try all sorts of plans. We've reached what, we believe, are balanced ways of dealing with allowances and chores. Both can be helpful in raising children today. An allowance gives children practical knowledge about the meaning and use of money. Doing chores teaches them that they can genuinely help their families and that others have needs, too. We can't return to a rural life where children were an essential part of the family economy. But we can, and should, teach them to be contributors to the family, not just consumers.

Don't mix allowances with chores. They serve two different purposes. If you tie your child's allowance to his chores, it becomes too complicated. What happens when he does part of his chores? Does he get part of his allowance? We believe children should not be paid for ordinary chores, although they can do extra jobs for money. *Connecting chores with money gives your children the idea that you have to pay them for helping the family.* I've often heard children say to their parents when they are asked to do something, "How much are you going to pay me?"

If you keep in mind that you're using an allowance to teach your kids about the proper use of money, and using chores to teach them about their responsibility to the family, it's easier to keep the family in balance.

Children doing chores has another benefit too; it takes some of the burden off already overworked parents. It's not a bad idea for children to know that the work they have to do around the house actually makes life a bit easier for mom and dad. We parents spend our lives trying to make our children's lives easier. At their own level, they can do the same for us. This is how we teach them to contribute to the welfare of the family, to be aware of others, and not to just be concerned for themselves — an essential ingredient in their spiritual development.

We have found the following plan helpful for allowances. Divide the allowance into four parts. We suggest that one part go into a long-term savings plan, something your child may want to save for in the future like a car or college — a big ticket item. Save a second part for special items like a video game or a toy, something your child wants to buy in a few weeks or a month. The third part goes for helping others who are less fortunate, maybe a good cause or a charity sponsored by the school or church. This gives your children the idea that they have a responsibility toward others who may be less fortunate. The last part they can "blow" just having fun — within reason, of course.

By dividing allowances into specific categories, you put the idea of money into balance for your children. You provide them practical experience with finances and budgeting. You're also helping them make long-term positive use of their money and to resist the destructive allure of instant gratification. You're teaching them how to make prudent budget decisions when they have to spend their own money for a toy they see on TV. Best of all, you're teaching them by sharing their wealth, they maintain psychological and spiritual balance.

Today, when greed is not only tolerated but even admired, learning concern for others is a critically-important lesson. Even small children of four or five can grasp the concept of sharing. Ask any preschool teacher. He or she will have lots of examples of children spontaneously sharing their toys or food with playmates. (Of course, they have opposite stories too.)

For many years our family has had the custom of adopting an economically less-fortunate family at Christmas, through a local non-profit organization called M.E.N.D. — "Meeting Each Need with Dignity." Each member of our family has to contribute some of his or her own money for the ingredients of our adopted family's Christmas dinner, as well as for their kids' presents. Our own children have developed the habit of saving a part of their allowance for this a few months before. One time Bonnie and I were surprised on our way back from delivering the packages to a family when our children agreed that that was what Christmas is all about.

Six Antidotes to Affluenza

Run a check on your own priorities and values to see what messages you're passing on to your kids:

1. Do you talk to them about future careers only on the basis of how much money they could make rather than on how fulfilled they would be?

2. Do you buy them things instead of spending time with them?

3. Are you doing tasks for them that they could do for themselves?

4. Do you ever have family fun without spending lots of money?

5. Are you making them aware of helping others who find themselves in less-fortunate circumstances?

6. Check to see if the material concerns in your life have thrown your family out of psychological and spiritual balance. We immunize our children from affluenza by protecting their souls from material excesses and, through firm, loving guidance, by encouraging them to take appropriate levels of responsibility for themselves.

CHAPTER V

Humor in the Family

It's much harder to do comedy than tragedy, for people laugh at different things, but all cry at the same thing.

Groucho Marx

To nurture the souls of our children, we need barrels of humor. When you see your teenage daughter drinking straight from the milk carton, or hear punk-rock music blaring out of your son's room, or discover your five-year-old practicing writing his name on your new wallpaper, you understand the wisdom of Groucho Marx's remark. Crying is often easier than laughing where our kids are concerned.

Humor is a first cousin of wisdom. It keeps us balanced. It prevents us from taking life too seriously. We especially need it for the transitions in life. Look at the funny stories and jokes about honeymoons, marriage, mid-life, tragedies, and death.

Right after World War I, an old woman was told by the authorities that the place she had lived in all of her life was no longer Russia. It was now part of Poland. "Thank God," she answered, "I always hated those Russian winters." In the face of great loss, she kept her balance through humor.

From a teenager's point of view, even suicide can be humorous. Take a story my fifteen-year-old neighbor Josh told me. A man was lying on a railroad track, munching a peanut butter and jelly sandwich. "What are you doing?" someone asked him.

"Committing suicide," he answered.

"If you're committing suicide, why do you have a sandwich in your hand?"

"In this country, before the train comes," he answered, "a man could starve to death."

Sadly, our society tends to downplay humor in raising children. We hear that children need to emphasize competition to be successful today; that they have to get a leg up on their peers; that the next generation will not do as well as we have done; and that college will be almost out of the reach of the middle class. Even at *Mommy and Me* classes, some mothers push their infants to crawl, sit and roll over better than their diapered, dribbling peers. Under pressure like this, laughter becomes a foreign language that serves no profitable purpose.

Bonnie and I have seen how important humor is, even in psychotherapy. Clients begin to get better when they see the humorous side of their problems. Several years ago, I was treating a very depressed man. At the beginning of one session, I saw him studying my feet, obviously puzzled. I looked down and saw that I had put on two different shoes, one black and the other brown — a mistake Bonnie would have no trouble believing. Realizing what I had done, I admitted my mistake. We both began to laugh at the incongruity of *me* — the doctor — supposedly having it more together than the client. Later, he told me he started his recovery from that session, when he saw I could laugh at myself.

A healthy sense of humor is as important to our children's growth as academic achievement, economical success or physical prowess. Because life has become so serious, we need more than ever to foster humor in ourselves, in our families, and in our children.

Whenever our whole family laughs together, it's like everyone hugging one another at the same time. There's a warm feeling of being connected. Even our seventy-pound dog Allie recognizes something special is going on, since she always comes bounding in whenever she hears us all laughing.

Parents can foster humor in the home. Susan, a mother of two boys, eight and ten, told us about the time her family was having rice bowls for dinner. She had warned them that round rice bowls could easily tip over if they were not careful. When she tried to spear a piece of chicken from the bottom of her bowl a little too enthusiastically, she missed the chicken, but managed to launch the bowl. As if in slow motion, Susan said, her bowl climbed into the air, then turned over as it made its way down, slowly showering grains of rice all over her before it somersaulted off the table to land upside-down on her lap. While her family stared wide-eyed, with open mouths in disbelief, Susan's warning echoed back to her. She burst out laughing. Since it now was safe, her kids joined her.

Susan's sense of humor taught her children a wonderful lesson. They returned it, too. After the laughter had died down, one of the boys looked at her. "How come you can laugh when you spill things, but you won't let us laugh when we do it?" he asked.

Susan's family is in good hands. She doesn't take life too seriously. She can laugh at herself. She sees the humor in the incongruity of a mother doing exactly the opposite of what she warned her kids about. Listen to your children. They help us stay balanced.

Humor also helps us through painful times. I'm from an Irish family. Relatives and friends of my family from different parts of the world come together to pay their respects to whichever member of our wide-ranging clan has died. Through their sad and funny stories they are able to soften the pain of loss. My memories of these times are a mixture of sadness and laughter. I've always had a wonderful time at wakes and funerals. My cousins and I would feast on the meats, Irish soda bread and desserts in the home where the deceased was being waked.

I remember at my Uncle Bill's wake, when no one was looking, we kids drained the last drops of beer from the discarded glasses. By the time my matriarchal Aunt Mary caught us and warned us that our dearly-departed Uncle was watching us from Heaven, we were too happy to feel guilty. Knowing Uncle Bill, he was too.

Unexpected humor softens tragedy. My cousin Irene tells of the time when she was attending the wake of her twenty-year-old girl-friend who had died suddenly from a brain tumor. After she said some prayers before the open casket, Irene offered her condolences to the grieving mother. Feeling awkward about what to say, she blurted out, "My, your daughter looks out of this world."

Irene felt her face turn beet-red. But, her inadvertent humor helped a grief-stricken mother find a smile at a most difficult time.

Our children give us lots of chances to laugh. Bonnie remembers, as a ten-year-old, coming through the kitchen and taking one of the freshly-baked cookies her mother had made for dinner. With an older brother and three younger siblings, when her mom asked her if she had taken the cookie, she'd (innocently) answer, "I just saw Rick coming out of the kitchen." When the mother asked Rick the same question, he would throw suspicion on another of his four siblings. Her mom and dad would then say, half-humorously to each other, "Ask a dumb question and you get a dumb answer." In the family, humor helps when you can't get the facts.

Humor keeps us from being pretentious and pompous. Sometimes the funniest incidents happen at the most sacred moments. Father Jim, a priest friend of mine, developed diarrhea the morning he was sched-uled to say Sunday Mass in front of a large congregation. As a precaution for a quick trip to the bathroom, he hid a roll of toilet paper underneath his long, flowing vestments. Fortunately, his body cooperated, and he was feeling much better when the sermon time came. He ascended the steep steps to the high, ornate pulpit. Forgetting about his upset stomach, he launched his sermon with a dramatic Moses-like sweep of his arms. He also launched the toilet paper. The roll shot out of his sleeve and skittered down the center aisle, turning the heads of the startled congregation as it unwound. "Well, so much for my attempt at dignity," Jim told them. The whole congregation exploded in laughter.

When Bonnie was a religious novice (a two-year training period before taking vows), her community of over one hundred sisters had all eaten refried beans for dinner. While they were saying community night prayers, a quickly-mounting number of the sisters were getting up and rushing out of the chapel. Bonnie couldn't figure out what was happening until the effects of the food poisoning hit her and she made her own beeline to the nearest bathroom. She can't remember when she felt so sick and laughed so hard at the same time. If there ever was a moment to lay to rest the popular belief that *nuns don't go to the bathroom,* this had to be it.

Humor shortens the distance between the lofty and the lowly by holding us back from either extreme. The serious is never far from the humorous; the humorous helps us deal with the serious.

Early Humor

Humor starts early. Preschool children use humor to begin the necessary process of becoming separate little people, different from their parents. It helps make the transitions they face less frightening. For example, your preschooler comes home from school and asks, "Why does the doggie cross the road?"

"I don't know, honey," you answer, "Why does the doggie cross the road?"

With an ear-to-ear smile, your child says, "Because it crosses the road!" and falls down laughing.

If you enjoy his joke and laugh with him, you help him to be separate from you and to feel good about the psychological distance between you. He knew something you didn't know. In fact, you probably wouldn't have guessed his answer in a million years.

On the other hand, if you say, "That's not so funny. Where's the punch line?" or, "Quit acting silly and start practicing your ABCs," then you may send your child the message that it's not okay to begin that difficult process of separating from you.

Small children have little or no privacy. We bathe them, wipe their little bottoms, dress them, and tell them what to do and what not to do. Humor helps the process of becoming separate little people. We have to validate our children's attempts to be funny, to let them experience surprising us because they know an answer we don't.

When you minimize the importance of early humor, it's as tragic as minimizing a child's attempts to learn to read. Reading helps develop the mind of a child. It's through reading that he will discover knowledge and make successful contact with the world outside his family. Humor will help develop his soul. It keeps him balanced by helping him joyfully embrace himself and the world.

Six-year-old Joey came in to see me at one of the schools where I am a consultant. His mother asked me to see him because she was worried about him crying at bedtime. He told me that he cried himself to sleep every night because his favorite uncle had died a few months before. When I asked him what was special about his uncle, he told me that Uncle Frank played with his *Star Wars* figures, told funny stories and jokes, and made him laugh.

"What were some of the jokes he told you?" I asked.

"Knock-knock jokes," he said.

"Tell me one," I said.

"Knock! Knock!"

"Who's there?" I asked, getting into the spirit.

"Tuba."

"Tuba who?"

"Tuba toothpaste," he answered, and started to laugh.

"Where does a two-thousand-pound gorilla sit in a movie theater?" he asked suddenly. His eyes were starting to glow.

"Where?" I asked.

"Anywhere he wants."

With each remembered story and joke, Joey began to perk up further. I suggested he think of the funny incidents with Uncle Frank at bedtime. Two weeks later, he came to see me again. He was grinning from ear to ear. "It worked," he said. "When I go to bed, I'm not sad anymore. I tell myself Uncle Frank's jokes and I always laugh." Humor helped him get back on track.

The next stage is bathroom jokes and sexual humor. Philip, a second-grade boy with sparkling eyes, asked that same ancient question: "Why does the chicken cross the road?" Only for Phillip, the hilarious answer was, "To go to the bathroom."

A single innocent word about the bathroom or private parts can send four- and five-year-olds into uncontrollable giggle fits. We parents have to be careful not to come down on them like avenging angels. This kind of humor is normal and natural. It's an indication that our children are becoming aware of their own bodies and the bodies of others. Such awareness can be an anxious and scary time for them. Humor diffuses the apprehension and uneasiness and helps them to keep their balance and not lose touch with their souls as they enter a new stage of life. Of course, we have to teach them what's appropriate and what's not — especially in front of our in-laws. However, realizing how essential humor can be at life's transitions, we have a better chance of keeping our own balance.

Teenage Humor

Humor takes a sarcastic turn during the teens. What parents haven't suffered through their teenager's sarcastic humor? "Are you going up to your room?" Mom asks her fourteen-year-old. "No, I'm going to Mt. Everest."

Sound familiar?

A fifteen-year-old boy who had his two front teeth knocked out in a football game had just come back from the dentist with temporary caps. Worried that he wouldn't be able to chew, his mother asked at dinner that night if he'd be able to swallow the pieces of steak he was shoveling into his mouth. "No," he answered, straight-faced, "I'm just storing them in my cheeks."

Teens become critical as they take a less-than-adoring look at their parents. They feel they know more than you. I saw a wonderful sign on a church marquee that hit the nail on the head: *Hire a teenager while they're sure they know everything.* Their sarcastic and somewhat put-down humor reflects this rocky time of their lives. You're not the only target; it's the way they talk to their friends, too.

At times, it may be better to overlook the sarcasm and to try to concentrate on the funny side, as long as it isn't clearly rude or disre-spectful. Rude or disrespectful is when your child calls you demeaning names, swears at you or disregards your authority. A parent should never tolerate that.

The other day our twenty-one-year-old son seemed to be in a par-ticular hurry to get out the door. "Are you rushing, dear?" Bonnie asked. He looked at her, hesitated a moment, and then answered, "No, I'm American."

Focus on your teenager's intention, not his words, which may not be as disrespectful as they sound. This will help you keep connected to his soul, rather than wringing his neck.

Teenagers are continually trying to throw others off balance. They trip the friend walking ahead of them and pounce on every mispro-nounced word a parent says. Teenage boys wrestle with each other at the drop of a hat. All of this is playful humor. In classical philosophy, humans are referred to as both *Homo Sapiens* (intellectual beings) and *Homo Ludens* (playful beings). We nurture our children by helping them develop both these essential human qualities.

We also nurture our children by being silly at times. Do the "old soft shoe" once in a while, sing like an opera star, or try to balance a coffee cup (make sure it's empty!) on your head. It helps create a relaxed atmosphere by inviting laughter.

Johnny Carson is a hero of a prominent psychiatrist friend of ours because the comedian was willing to let a straw dangle from his nostril on national TV. This doctor knows what balance is.

Sometimes a sense of humor gets us through embarrassing situa-tions. We were in a restaurant with our two children when they were eight and six. As you may have noticed, children at this age don't mod-ulate their voices. We were talking about a couple who recently had a baby. My then eight-year-old daughter, at megaphone volume, asked, "How does a woman start to have a baby inside her?"

In our soft, controlled, adult voices, we whispered an answer that obviously didn't satisfy Kathleen. "No, I want to know exactly how it happens," she insisted.

Somehow, she managed to get still louder. By this time, the crowded restaurant had taken on the respectful silence of a church as all the patrons waited for our wise response. I decided to let Bonnie handle this one. I can't remember what she said. I only recall wishing restaurants had fire drills.

Pregnancy tends to be a dangerous subject around kids of this age. Friends of ours were at dinner with their two children, ages nine and six, and the father's very proper parents. During the course of the conversation, the *P-word* came up. The nine-year-old daughter said, "I have a question."

The girl's mother, a clinical psychologist who prided herself on her openness with her children, was glad for the chance to impress her in-laws. "Yes, dear, what is it?" the mother asked. With everyone's eyes upon her, the daughter asked, "How does the penis stay hard?"

Forks dropped on the table. The grandparents felt the need to cough simultaneously. To this day, our psychologist friend doesn't know what she answered. She only remembers her husband quickly offering wine to his teetotalling parents.

Take a careful look at your family. Is humor an integral part of your family life? If it is, the members of your family probably feel close to each other, and you're well on the road to balance. If not, why not? Are you overemphasizing school achievement or activities? When I was in the Carmelite Order, we would have an annual retreat to re-establish life's priorities. While your family probably can't get away for an extended retreat, you might have a meeting to discover where the family is out of balance.

Humorless people tend to be overly serious, defensive about their own mistakes, and controlling. When parents fit this description, children experience a lot of tension. If a child can't laugh at the silly mistakes his parents make, he won't be able to laugh at himself.

Whenever Bonnie and I visit a home without humor, we can feel the coldness and distance between the family members. In family therapy, we sometimes surprise the family members by initially downplaying the problem they came in for and asking them about the funny things that go on in the family. If they all start remembering funny incidents and begin laughing, we know that this family will get back on track with a minimum of our help. On the contrary, if the family has little or no examples of family humor, and sit staring into space, we know our work with them won't be easy.

Four Helpful Hints

1. Pay attention to what your kids say.

Often, their remarks are funny. As all parents know, kids say things once and once only. If you are not listening carefully, you may miss their humor.

2. Check your own sense of humor.

Are you too serious? What makes you laugh? Discover your funny-bone.

3. Try to be aware of the particular sense of humor each of your children has.

Is it subtle and dry, easily missed if you're not paying close attention? Or is it boisterous, open and silly, hitting you in the face like a cream pie?

4. Did something funny happen to you during the day?

Share it with your family. Show them parents have a sense of humor. Dinner can be a wonderful time to have each member share strange and funny things that happened to them. When our children were little, we had a custom where each of us had to tell a story or incident that happened during the day. Frequently, humor played a part in what we had experienced that day.

Humor is intimately connected to the soul.

CHAPTER VI

Taking Charge In Your Home

The people turn to a benevolent ruler as water flows downward.

Mencius

When I take our dog Allie for a walk, I come out in the yard with her blue leash in my hand. The sight puts her beside herself with joy, leaping and jumping with such enthusiasm that I can hardly fasten it to her dog collar. Once the collar is on, she bounds out of the gate with me holding on for dear life. Yet if I open the gate without putting on her leash, she won't run out. If I accidentally drop the leash while we are walking, she stops immediately and waits for me to pick it up before taking off again like a canine bronco.

Allie is smart. She knows she can be free to romp and play only if I keep her safe. Kids are like Allie. They feel free and elated only if they know we are guiding them.

To understand how important feeling safe is for children, imagine you're on an airplane about to take off. You're in your seat, your belt fastened, seat in an upright position, tray secure. You hear the engines roar and feel the powerful thrust of the aircraft as it races down the runway and lifts into the sky. The other passengers fall silent in that slight case of nerves that seems to characterize take-offs everywhere. The plane levels off, finally. Talking eases the nervousness and you start to relax again.

"Welcome, ladies and gentlemen," the pilot's voice says, "to Flight 789 from Los Angeles to Chicago. Flying time will be about three hours and twenty minutes. Our cruising altitude will be about . . . Ah, let me see. About . . ." The pilot's voice breaks off abruptly. There are several seconds of silence. Passengers and crew look quizzically at each other when the voice resumes hesitantly, "Well, I'm not sure about the cruising altitude. I don't know", you hear him say (to the co-pilot, you hope). "What do you think, Frank? Maybe we should ask the passengers to help us decide." Your newly-acquired calm would be instantly shattered.

This is what children experience when they sense adults are not in charge. The circumstances may vary in families, but every child who has to take on responsibility beyond his capacity suffers from the same pervasive insecurity. It feels to them like the ground they're standing on keeps moving. A child finds it hard to keep his psychological and spiritual balance in a home where the parents fail to take charge.

Single parents and dual-career parents have a particularly difficult time today. They may be obliged to leave their youngsters home alone between 3 and 5 p.m. Extended families of aunts, cousins, grandparents, who filled in for a missing parent, have all but disappeared. The cohesive neighborhood where children were both cared for and disciplined has become as outdated as knickers.

Both Bonnie and I grew up in neighborhoods of large families. The streets we knew were safe and filled with kids. My mother simply opened the back door and called me (I won't say how many times) in for meals. I went to elementary and high school within walking distance of my home.

Because the environment is more dangerous, children, nowadays, are virtual prisoners in their homes. They wait for their tired parents to run them to soccer, ballet, karate, or friends' houses. They have to be driven to school — even if the school is within walking distance.

All of this puts parents under great pressure. They look for any available help, sometimes turning to their children for reassurance, or even advice. It's hard to resist such a temptation, especially for single moms and dads. Being the only adult in the home with accidents, sickness and all the unexpected things that happen to children, a single parent often needs someone to bounce ideas off of. But the whole family loses its balance when we make our children our confidants.

The result? Increasingly, we see children acting as if the family were a democracy where every member, regardless of age has an equal voice. A ten-year-old feels he has as much right to decide his bedtime as his parents do. A sixteen-year-old tells her parents she will make her own decisions about her life from now on. We may have gone too far in allowing our kids to express whatever they feel like expressing, whenever they feel like expressing it. We hear parents complain, "My kids are so disrespectful to me. I would have been scared to death to talk to my parents that way." When she was young, Bonnie can remember her parents telling her "get that look off your face."

Sam Levinson, a popular comic in the 1950s, told about his own family when he was a child. Occasionally, when his working-class father came home in the evening, he slapped the first child he saw. He figured one of the seven must have done something to deserve the whack, so he'd save himself the time of having to search out the particulars.

We don't want to return to those days. However, neither do our children have the right to treat us disrespectfully. We must show our children we are in charge. The family loses its balance when no one is clearly in control. Children who can count on the wise leadership of their parents develop calmness and trust that prematurely-independent youngsters lack. Parental leadership is the foundation for the psychological and spiritual balance of the child. In such an environment, the soul is nurtured.

Children can't learn to trust when they are insecure. A family in which no one is in charge is like the pilot asking for help from his passengers, or our dog Allie not knowing what to do when her leash falls off. Children need to be protected from their own undeveloped judgment — and, at a fundamental level, they know it. The odds of kids making serious mistakes are greater when they can't rely on their parents' guidance. Pick up a newspaper any day of the week. You'll find too many tragic examples of kids who, left on their own, end up hurting themselves or others.

The growing attitude of society toward trying children as adults in the courts is a good example of our expecting them to act like adults in a society that is itself out of control. We adults don't have the answers to the problems of violence and juvenile crime. Lacking the wisdom, we blame the children. By definition, when we want to treat youngsters of twelve and thirteen as adults, we admit we are no longer in control. Blaming children is another way of looking to them for help in solving their problems.

Middle or late teens, who have been allowed to make too many decisions prematurely, expect to decide even major issues without the "interference" of their parents. Bonnie and I see teenagers in our office who tell us bluntly that they will decide what to do no matter what their parents say. With a premature air of sophistication, they tell us, "I know myself and what I need better than anyone."

We are always saddened when we hear this, knowing the perils and pitfalls that life puts in the path of each of us. If they are unwilling to let us help them as counselors, we tell teenagers that we'll keep them in our prayers, that if they don't want the adults in their world to help, we'll ask God to step in for us. Surprisingly, we've yet to have a teen reject the offer. Instead, these wanna-be adults express appreciation when they learn they are being prayed for, even if they have no religious affiliation of their own. Somehow the idea that someone is praying for them seems comforting. Prayer seems to touch them deeply; it seems to nurture their souls.

In some ways we have only ourselves to blame when our children take over their lives too early. Some parents too often let their four-year-olds decide at which restaurant the family will eat, or permit their elementary-school children to choose their own bedtimes. Teachers tell us some students refuse to do assignments because they've decided the work is meaningless. One principal of a private school told us about a six-year-old who was sent to her because he repeatedly disrupted the class by talking out loud. The boy entered her office without knocking, sat down and stated, "I have my rights." She said it took her a few minutes to recover before she informed him, in no uncertain terms, that the school has its rights too.

It's no surprise that teenagers, long-accustomed to making their own decisions prematurely, will feel entitled to make major decisions. For the sake of both parents and children, mom and dad need to reclaim their parental authority. It's the only way to get the family back on track.

Moral Authority

Of all the ways parents can exercise control over their children, we have found what we call "moral authority" the most effective in guiding our children and keeping that close connection we and our children need. Moral authority is what enables parents to be sure that a child will obey a serious command, no matter how angry and intense the child is. Moral authority means the child *obeys,* not primarily out of fear, but out of a fundamental respect for his parents. He can clench his fist, puff up his chest, grunt at ear-shattering volume, or stomp away, muttering fiercely. Parents, who have moral authority, know the bravado is for show. Deep down, the child has too much respect for the parents *not* to obey them. Parents who have developed moral authority are in charge in their home.

There is no mystery in developing moral authority. It comes from being responsible parents, from respecting children as individuals who will someday have lives separate from the parents, from not using their children for their own needs, from modeling the values that they want their children to develop, and from not blocking their children from going through the necessary steps of their physical and psychological development. In short, moral authority comes from being a committed parent.

Paradoxically, parents with moral authority tend to be more flexible. Their children feel safer and even enjoy greater privileges. Such parents distinguish reacting between minor and major issues. They don't sweat the little things. They save the "big guns" for the "big" problems. As a result, they are not fearful that their children will go out of control.

Frank and Joanne grounded their fifteen-year-old son Jason for breaking his curfew without a good reason. Jason, of course, thought it was unjust. He stomped up to his room grumbling about how unfair they were. The parents thought they caught a few words that sounded like, "They can't make me. I'll go out if I want to," as they heard the door slam.

Mom and Dad overlooked Jason's verbal bravado and slammed door. For them, the important thing was they knew he'd accepted being grounded. Their confidence in their own authority kept them balanced. They didn't "sweat" the slammed door.

Were Frank and Joanne not sure Jason would accept his punishment, the slammed door could have sent his parents over the top. They might have blown this minor infraction out of proportion. That kind of overreaction could have thrown the whole incident out of balance, leaving both parents and son frustrated.

Parents who allow themselves to overreact on the small things come across as unpredictable. Frequently, these parents' reactions are more a response to their own emotional moods and personal stresses, rather than the actual incident with their child. The severity of their reaction depends not on the severity of the transgression but on how well — or badly — the day has gone. The kids simply can't anticipate how Mom and Dad will react to a given situation. "Sometimes," a child will say, "I do something, and my parents act like it's okay. Other times I do the same thing, and they go bonkers."

James Wilson, a social scientist from the Claremont Colleges, thinks that children who live in severely-dysfunctional families where their parents are involved in drugs, alcohol or other criminal activity, do not learn that there are predictable consequences to their actions. From their earliest years, these children experience life as a capricious system that doesn't depend upon the good or bad things they do. They don't learn to make a connection between their actions and consequences, for themselves or others.

Families work best when parents put down clear rules. Being in charge doesn't mean we are cruel or self-serving. We maintain a loving, temporary control because that's what our children need to feel protected. We say *temporary,* since our goal as parents is to prepare our kids to eventually leave home and — hopefully — become responsible adults in their turn. The souls of our children are free to fly only if they have been carried on the wings of their parents while they were young.

CHAPTER VII

Eleven Guideposts
on the Road to Balance

I pray Heaven to bestow the best of blessings on this house and all who shall hereafter inhabit it. May none but the honest and wise ever rule under this roof.

John Adams

How do you stay in charge in your home without resorting to *Gestapo* tactics? How do you maintain control while enabling all your family members to keep their psychological and spiritual balance? How do you create an atmosphere in your home that helps you nurture the souls of your children? Besides humor and the immunization of our children against affluenza, we've found the following tips helped us in our own family as well as in the many families we've worked with over the years.

1. Listen to Your Children's Version

A Rabbi was holding court, hearing the complaints of two women against each other. The Rabbi listened intently to the first, and persuaded by her tears, said, "You are right." The other woman shouted, "Wait, you have not heard me." He listened to her also and, again persuaded, said, "You are right."

The Rabbi's wife said in a perplexed voice, "How can they both be right?" And he replied, "You are right, too."

This little story has helped us to wait until we get input from our children about what and why they did something. It taught us that if two things are contradictory, one doesn't have to be true and the other false. Maybe both have some claim to the truth. This attitude has often kept us from jumping to impetuous conclusions.

I used the Rabbi's story in a talk to teachers. Several weeks later, a high-school principal who had attended wrote to tell me this story had changed her life. Now, she continued, when anyone comes into the office she tells them they are *right*. "When I begin this way," she added, "they feel understood, and I don't have to pretend I've got the wisdom of Solomon. Best of all, we reach solutions more quickly."

Kids constantly tell Bonnie and me that their parents don't even *listen* to them, much less try to understand their side of a problem. Too often we parents automatically conclude that whatever conflict we have with our kids, we are *right* and they are *wrong*. Yet I don't remember God bestowing the gift of infallibility on us.

Usually, the truth lies somewhere in the middle. Ed was furious last fall when his fifteen-year-old daughter, Amy, came home forty-five minutes late for her curfew. Waiting for her, his mood jumped from fear that she had been in an accident to belief that she just didn't care. He was so agitated when she finally came home (in a car he had never seen before) that he screamed at her about how worried he was, and how disrespectful she was. He didn't give her a chance to tell what had happened. Result: Amy went to bed angry because he wouldn't listen to her explanation. She was scared because she didn't know what punishment she'd get the next day. And Ed? He could hardly sleep the whole night.

The next morning, after he'd calmed down, he found out that his daughter had decided not to stay with the friends with whom she had gone to the party because they were talking about smoking marijuana. "That didn't sound cool to me," she said.

Instead, she'd asked another group if she could get a ride home with them. When she got in the car, she found out the driver had to drop off other kids before he could take her home. "I knew you would be worried," she said, "but there was no car phone, and I didn't know the other kids well enough to ask them to call from their homes."

Ed went on to describe how he felt like digging a deep hole and jumping into it. "Not only was my daughter concerned, but she showed good judgment in avoiding marijuana." I told Bill to keep the Rabbi's story in his hip pocket. It will keep him balanced.

2. Calm vs. Catastrophic

The media's constant imposition of "good life" images have changed our idea of what constitutes success. Parents of the past were less focused on material or academic success. They also didn't feel so responsible for how their children eventually turned out. But our families are smaller than those of a generation ago. In families with six, seven or eight children, parents were proud if just one or two of their kids did well. "Eileen and Jimmy have done great in their work and marriage," parents would say. "The rest of our children are still struggling, especially Jack and Mary. But they'll make it with the help of God." Back in the 50s parents could still say that without feeling guilty.

Now, with families averaging one to three children, parents invest far more of themselves in trying to make each child successful. Consequently, they may put pressure on children that was virtually unthinkable a generation ago. They also may pressure themselves for ensuring the success of *all* their children. The result is that children are under a microscope, and so even a minor incident can cause parents to project a catastrophic future.

Harry, a normal twelve-year-old, had a room that could best be described as an example of what an 8.5 earthquake might do. His bed was somewhere under the *Notre Dame* blanket, which was itself under his school books, which were under the pizza box, which sat on top of the golf clubs and clean unfolded laundry, which was — you get the idea. If you searched hard enough, I'm sure you could have found the carpet.

Harry's mother, Katherine, had been telling him to clean up the mess for weeks with no success. Finally, exasperated, she said, "How many times have I told you to clean up your room? If you are so sloppy now, how do you expect to keep a roommate in college? No one will want to live with you. Do you think you'll ever get married if you're going to keep your house like you keep your room? And who will want to share a room with you in the old folks' home?" Mom went from her 12-year-old's messy quarters to predicting a lonely senior citizen. *That's catastrophic thinking!*

Here's another example. Your seven-year-old daughter comes home with a note from the second-grade teacher telling you she was benched for pushing another child. You look at her, but your imagination races ahead. *My God, she's only seven and she's already in trouble. I'll bet she's another Aunt Myrtle* (the wild one of the family). *She'll probably have a frequent-visitors' pass to the Principal's office. Juvenile Hall by high school. God, help me! I can see her in prison blues already.*

Sound familiar? You're reacting not to the small, real infraction but to an imagined life of crime. As a result, you may never remember to ask her what *caused* her to push the other little girl. You may never realize you need to teach her non-physical ways of resolving conflict. There's another term for this kind of thinking, by the way. It's called "self-fulfilling prophecy."

We have to reign in our exaggerated fears that something "bad" will happen to our kids. We can't let fear be the dominating motive in protecting our children. Instead, we need to hone in on the present incident as it happened — not on some possible future calamity. If your fear of a catastrophe happening to your child from a class outing or from contact sports is greater than your joy of watching him participate, then you are communicating fear. Unfortunately, it's easy to fall into this trap today. The nightly news is designed to play on our fears. To sell "air time" our "news" stations create the impression that disaster lurks outside our front doors. They urge us to stay alert twenty-four hours a day, seven days a week, and three-hundred-sixty-five days a year. Everything, they warn us — from the food we eat to the air we breathe — is a potential calamity. We are bombarded by imminent disaster every time we tune in.

My own sampling of one local news program recently brought this point home to me. The lead story featured the sale of contaminated foods at local supermarkets. The second news item "revealed" billions of microscopic organisms cavorting in our bed linens. After that came the neighborhood murders, drive-by shootings on the freeways, the release of a convicted pedophile who was about to move into everybody's neighborhood. The program closed with an exposé of scam artists preying on older, unsuspecting homeowners.

No wonder we walk around unbalanced. No wonder our souls (which thrive in a quiet, unhurried, and balanced environment) are hidden from us.

There are two ways in which we can control catastrophic thinking. These methods keep us more psychologically and spiritually balanced. They facilitate our search for our souls and the souls of our children. One is the cognitive-behavioral approach, which has been used successfully by mental health professionals in psychotherapy. The second is straight-forward common sense: keep calm.

Cognitive-Behavioral Theory teaches us to control self-defeating or negative thoughts by consciously putting positive thoughts in their place. The theory is that *we can't hold positive and negative thoughts in our minds simultaneously*. If we assume something bad will happen, chances are better than average that we will behave in a manner that makes our assumptions come true. *Thought influences behavior.* That's what self-fulfilling prophecy means.

The cognitive-behavioral approach says that *our beliefs and habits of thinking are a major source of our distress.* In other words, if we believe something negative about ourselves or about our children, then we'll act as if our belief were "Gospel truth." And because we — or our children — respond to our actions, we'll keep proving how right our beliefs are.

John, a twenty-eight-year-old single medical research-scientist, was very lonely. However, he avoided going out to social functions because he was convinced that his shyness and his work as a researcher were an immediate turn-off to others, especially young women. He defeated himself before he even stepped out of the house. As a result of John's own thinking, he always found himself mute and alone at gatherings, his catastrophic expectations having come true once again.

John came to see me because he was tired of being alone and didn't have a clue about what to do. I pointed out to him how his mind directs his whole being in such a negative way that he's probably giving off the message by his posture, facial expression, and voice that says, "Avoid me. I'm boring." I suggested that he go to the next social function with the idea that he will at least enjoy the food, even if no one talks to him. I also suggested that he remind himself to smile, stand straight and look like he is enjoying himself.

John's new social approach didn't produce any miracles. Yet, *slowly* he began to see that his own thinking had trapped him in loneliness. After several months of soul-searching and practice with me, he began to connect to others and feel better about himself. He no longer assumed that others automatically found him boring.

The constant theme Liliana heard from her father was "You're stupid. You'll never amount to anything in life." Even when she occasionally did something well, her father either paid no attention or told her she had "lucked out." Now, at thirty-three, she listed a litany of job and relationship failures that seemed to prove to her how effective her father's prediction was.

She came to see Bonnie to begin the painful process of recognizing that she had taken over her father's catastrophic thinking about herself.

She "knew" that every new job and every new relationship would turn sour sooner or later. And she was always right. She spent many months in therapy before she finally began to emerge as a separate person and not as the victim of her father's curse. She slowly took more control of her thoughts until, like the tiny, fragile buds of a new flower, she began to let optimistic thoughts linger in her mind. With this hope, she experienced the joy of living for the first time in her life. She'd begun to nurture her soul.

The second way of controlling catastrophic thinking is staying calm. As anyone with a healthy two-year-old knows, this is no easy task. Yet, if you lose control, forget about resolving the issue. Put the problem back on the shelf until both you and your child are calm.

Eleven-year-old Richard was suspended from school for being with a group of boys who wrote some graphic graffiti on the bathroom wall. *He* didn't write anything, but his dad lost his cool when he heard the news, saying he could never trust his son again.

In reality, Richard was a great kid who rarely got into trouble. Of course, Dad didn't mean what he had said. He had lost his balance. Had he kept his cool (and his mouth shut for a few minutes), he would have had a better chance of putting the whole incident into perspective. Then, Dad could have put his energy into the more important issue of teaching his son how to handle peer pressure. Instead his father blew it with his catastrophic reaction.

Like most children, Richard accepted what his father said literally. What a parent says has the power to comfort or to wound. Although the intemperate words of a coach, teacher or neighbor can produce distress, it is usually the searing, cruel utterances of a parent that cause the most lasting pain. As parents, we would do well to realize how powerful our words are in the minds and souls of our children.

None of us can go through life without losing our self-control once in a while, so when you get really tense, when you realize you're on the edge of losing control, admit it. Tell your children that you're too "worked up" to think clearly, that you need to quiet down before continuing. Admit that *you* need a time-out this time. Even if you have to leave the room or take a short walk, you'll have a greater chance of resolving the issue once you've calmed down. While your blood's pounding in your ears, you have no chance at all.

The same goes for your child. If your preteen or teen starts screaming, tell him you'll discuss the issue when he is calm. We remember our children's struggles to regain some semblance of control so they could come back to argue their cases. If children know that all discussion stops the minute one person loses control, they will make an heroic effort to calm down. A friend of mine graphically described his angry son breathing deeply, steam coming out of both ears, eyes flashing like a dragon getting ready to spit fire. It always took the boy a while, but he would recover after a few minutes, and then he and his father would resume the discussion. Dad could tell that his son felt better for getting back in control, especially when he sometimes was able to convince his parents that their position was unfair. It was through his occasional, hard-won, honest victory, that his parents taught him the value of keeping calm.

Unfortunately the media, especially in its sports coverage, sometimes fails to teach children the value of self-control. Professional hockey openly allows two players to "slug it out" in full view of fans while the game itself is interrupted. Minor punishments are imposed upon major sports figures for fighting during a game. This tacit acceptance makes the need for parents to teach and especially to model self-control even more urgent today.

In two-parent families, it's helpful to ask the less-agitated parent to take over while the more agitated parent tries to regain his/her composure. Bonnie and I did this, a lot. I have to admit that I had to ask her more often than she had to ask me — testosterone rides again!

Single moms and dads have a harder time of it, since they have to face the difficult times alone. If you're a single parent, try to call a friend. Take a "time-out" to recover your equilibrium. Even a short break on the telephone with an empathic friend can help you wade back into whatever thorny issue has you and your child at odds.

At one of our recent talks, a mother told us she had attended one of our lectures five years before. She'd begun then to use time-outs for herself whenever she reached the edge. She said she couldn't count the number of times she kept things from exploding by this simple, common sense technique. She added, "I keep my balance better."

One way children learn to be calm is by watching their parents stay calm under duress. Remember, you are your child's first definition of adult behavior. Parents need to contain their own feelings before they can control their children's. I can't tell you how often parents come to our office complaining that their children are rude, use foul language, and lose control at the drop of a hat. It doesn't take long to discover the kids are copying what they see at home. Parents scream "Don't scream!" at their children. "Don't hit your brother," a father says, while he's spanking his child. "Don't you call me a so-and-so," a mother yells, "you little so-and-so!" It'd be funny, if it wasn't so destructive.

A child needs to watch mom and dad contain their own anger, to see them avoid doing destructive things like hitting, or smashing the wall, or breaking things when they are upset. Look at the lessons our children learn from major sports' figures. As I write this, two Los Angeles newspapers, as well as local TV, blare the story of two professional baseball players having to be physically restrained from going after their manager for taking them out of a game. The attitudes of "In your face!" or "Make my day!" have become out-of-balance mantras that damage the soul.

In such an environment, it's easy for us to excuse our own lapses. A parent can feel justified for his own childish behavior because of the behavior of his child. "He made me so mad," he says, "I just lost it." What the child needs is for the parents to accept the responsibility for their own behavior.

Yet remaining calm is not easy, but we have to keep trying. We're parents. We have an adult duty and responsibility for the lives we have created. Just as the police are obliged to stay calm and maintain control in the face of outrageous behavior, so parents are obliged to remain in control regardless of our children's behavior. It's part of the job. In fact, we parents have the added obligation to intervene when one of our children is on the verge of losing control. This is called *containment of feelings*. Our children depend upon our wisdom to keep them and ourselves under control. We can't do that if we fail to control both our anger and our tendency toward catastrophic reactions.

Of course, not all catastrophes are imagined. We live in Northridge, a suburb of Los Angeles. At 4:32 a.m., on January 17, 1994, a 6.9 earthquake immortalized our sleepy bedroom community. It was the costliest natural disaster in the history of our country. Along with thousands of other families, the four of us were violently thrown out of bed that dark winter morning. Stumbling over upended couches, knocked-over cabinets and broken glass, Bonnie and I desperately called out our children's names as we searched for them, praying that no one had been hurt. Thank God, we found them rattled but safe and sound.

What I remember most vividly was the sound of the earth moving, like a runaway train racing through our home, the crashing of glass from the kitchen and cabinets, and the repeated aftershocks. We heard explosions all around as power transformers blew throughout the Valley. Through our darkened windows, we saw fires shooting up into the sky. *Now that was a catastrophe!*

Fearing an explosion in our own backyard, we rushed outside to shut off our gas lines. After that, we joined our neighbors in checking the lines of other houses, making sure everyone's gas line was turned off. This was our first step in regaining as much control over our lives as possible in the face of such a major disaster. We quickly realized that we had to stay calm or we would lose our balance. We could not correctly assess our danger, take the needed actions and work together without being calm.

Over the next few weeks, we learned to survive without running water, electricity and such normal conven-iences of city living as showers and flushing toilets. It was a hands-on refresher course in the difference between catastrophic thinking and the "real thing." The real thing jolts you back to life's basic priorities, including your religious beliefs. Remember that old saying "There are no atheists in fox holes!" It's true. I prayed more during those early earthquake days than I had since resigning from the Carmelites.

People who have a strong faith in God or in a higher power seem to have an added resource in controlling their catastrophic thinking.

Susan, a good friend of ours who has a strong religious faith, tells us that when her older teenage children go out at night or off on trips she puts their safety in God's hands. "I let go," she says, "and let God take over." Susan's ability to find peace in this way grows out of her connection to her soul. It keeps her balanced.

3. Negative Connections

When our children were little, I came home from work, walked in the door, and began turning off all the lights in the empty rooms. I got angrier with each light I counted. I greeted my children with a lecture on the waste of electricity. Usually they looked at me as if I were speaking Quechua, the language spoken in the mountains of Peru. One day after my lecture fell flatter than usual, Bonnie pointed out to me that my first evening encounter with our children was negative and critical. This set the tone for the rest of the evening. So I tried a different approach. I still counted the lights (as my father did before me), but *first* I greeted my children warmly with hugs and kisses, and asked them about their day. Then I told them about the lights. I can't say I ever solved the electric problem, but my relationship with my children noticeably improved. They returned the hugs and kisses, which made it easier for me to pay the electric bill.

In our talks and workshops, we ask parents to estimate the percentage of negative interactions that go on at home. Many admit to seventy-five or eighty percent. Parents constantly find fault with their children. They have invested so much emotional energy in them. Yet, negativity begets negativity. When we concentrate only on the blunders and mistakes of our kids, we begin to develop a radar-like system in which every misdeed makes a blip on our screen. It becomes increasingly harder for us to see our children's positive qualities, and they sense we are impossible to please. The whole household tilts toward the negative, leaving balance by the wayside.

An all-too-frequent lament Bonnie and I hear from young people is that their parents never comment on the good things they do. Of course, we know that children exaggerate, just as we know they almost never admit their own faults. (Who does?) But they have a point. When parents constantly highlight negative behavior, they are feeding their children's negative self-image. I am not saying that you should never criticize your children. They need to hear how their actions affect themselves and others. What I do say is to keep a balance between criticism and praise. A child who feels that he is valued and pleasing to his parents can listen to a reprimand without feeling devastated. He knows he's earned the criticism just as he knows he's earned the praise he's received. But a child who hears almost nothing but censure and reproach can be shattered by the slightest reproof. He has no emotional armor of praise to offset it.

We recommend that children learn that each new day is a fresh start — that the mistakes and problems of yesterday are not carried over to haunt our children for weeks on end. This attitude toward life will help them remain optimistic about the future and not become too discouraged about their past mistakes.

Here's a handy guide to check if what we say to ourselves or to others increases or decreases feelings of self-worth. If you average saying positive things two out of three times, you're increasing self-esteem. If two out of three times, you emphasize the negative, you are diminishing self-worth. This is true whether you are talking to yourself or to another.

The second part of the guide is that not saying something negative is better for self-esteem than saying something positive. Sounds like what my mother used to tell me when I was a boy, "Tom, if you can't say something nice about someone, don't say anything at all."

Sometimes, in our effort to give our children a strong sense of self, we may minimize criticism or exaggerate a positive quality. When his child doesn't make a school team or isn't picked for a part in a play, a parent may say, "I don't know why they didn't pick you. You are the best player on the team." Such statements ring false. Most children are realistic about their abilities. In fact, they tend to be overly critical of themselves. What a child needs at such a time is for her parent to guide her away from an internal dialogue that may have her already convinced she is inadequate. This is what Nora's mother did in the following story.

Nora had been practicing all summer to make her high-school cheerleading team. She and her friend Lily faithfully went through the routines for hours each day. Several times a week they went over their routines with a former head cheerleader at their school. When the try-outs were held, both girls were very hopeful because of all the work they had done. As Nora's Mom tells the story, her daughter came home crushed. Lily made the squad but Nora didn't.

Nora started the negative monologue: "I must be a klutz. I can't do anything well. How can I face my friends? They'll all think I'm a loser. Lily won't be my friend anymore. How can I ever go back to school? I wasn't good enough to be a cheerleader. Maybe I'm not good enough to be anything."

Nora's Mom was very wise. She let her daughter spill out her feelings of devastation without trying to make her feel better right away. Mom didn't put the judges or the other girls down by saying, "They must be fools not to pick you because you're so much better than Lily or a lot of the other girls." She simply held her sobbing daughter for a long time without saying anything. After Nora's sobs had subsided, Mom told her she understood how disappointed Nora was after dreaming about it and working so hard for such a long time. The mother later told me how close she felt to her daughter. "It seemed like I was connected to her very soul." With such a deep connection, Nora's Mom was able to guide her daughter through those turbulent moments back to a more positive self-image.

Sit down with your partner and check to see how much negative interaction there is between you and your children. Make a conscious effort to turn this around so that the atmosphere of your home is more positive than negative, more balanced than imbalanced.

Spouses can help one another by pointing out the unnecessary negative comments each makes to the children. I know, at times, I emphasize the negative without realizing it until Bonnie brings it to my attention. Often the observing partner gets a clearer picture of what's going on than the one who's speaking.

Once in a while, ask your children, "What are the positive things you think I like about you?" A father tried this and was surprised when his child couldn't think of anything his father liked about him. "That taught me a lesson on how critical I must have been to my son," the father added sadly.

4. The Big Picture

You come home after a long and difficult day at the office. Entering the house, you find all the lights on and the dog, who is supposed to be confined in the kitchen, wandering around loose. There's a fresh canine body imprint on the new leather living room couch. On the message board there is a note from your sixteen-year-old son: *Mom and Dad, I went to Bill's house. The number is 773-9999. Love, Bobby.*

Your first impulse is anger at seeing the lights on and the imprint of the nomadic dog. However, if you factor in the note and the fact that your son has not burned down the house or thrown a party, and that, in general, he is a good kid, your response will be better balanced. This is looking at the "big picture" and not just narrowly focusing on the lapses.

The big picture is essential in keeping your balance. Our kids are walking disasters. When they are little, children spill milk and write on freshly-painted walls. As they grow, so does the magnitude of their blunders. It's so easy to concentrate only on what they do wrong because they offer us an abundant menu of accidents, problems and miscalculations.

It's too easy for us to turn into detectives, searching out our child's tiniest lapses. Yet, if we concentrate on the negative, we can actually contribute to their making more mistakes. This type of focusing puts the whole family on alert and makes everyone uptight. The result is that our children make avoidable mistakes, as do we. We all perform better if we relax.

Marge told us that her teenage daughter, Samantha, would leave five or six towels on the bathroom floor after showering. Repeated requests had zero effect. Marge had a choice of blowing up, yelling or giving her usual lecture. However, she remembered our advice about the big picture. She assessed Sam on a larger scale: no drugs, no alcohol, no cigarettes, good grades and friends who are decent and respectful. Overall, she was a great kid. Mom decided that maybe she herself could pick up the towels. She saw that this approach kept her focused on the important aspects and helped her distinguish between significant and insignificant issues. Marge kept her balance.

Jack was a nineteen-year-old freshman at a local community college. Since the college was a half-hour freeway drive away, his parents decided to let him drive the new family car instead of his own clunker. It was safer. Jack's Dad laid down what he thought were reasonable rules about not making the car his bedroom annex — a story only fully understood by parents of teenage boys. But several weeks in a row when Dad wanted to use the car, he found gum wrappers, gym shoes, school books, CDs, old sweat socks and a few downright unidentifiable objects in the car. Dad blew a gasket. He chewed Jack out like a Marine drill sergeant training a raw recruit. When Dad righteously finished, Jack laid out his case. This was semester exam week; he continued to work twenty hours at his job; the assignments for the voluntary program to help him transfer to a major four-year college were due that week; he had a dental appointment which had taken a lot longer than he had anticipated; and he was trying to redo an English paper to get a better grade.

When Dad realized that his son's plate was overloaded, he understood why the messy car was low on his son's priority list. He told me he regretted having come down on Jack so heavily. We parents can too easily forget the multiple issues our children may be dealing with. When our children let go of an item of minor importance (at least to them!), it may be their way of keeping balance. We can safeguard our own equilibrium by having the wisdom of understanding their choice.

The big picture is a useful yardstick for us to measure our responses to our children, our spouses, our friends and ourselves. How many of us can say we are up to speed on every facet of our lives? If you grade yourself on all levels of your life and give yourself an A+, you are probably on the verge of burn-out or of becoming delusional. We may get an A- in our job, a B+ in housekeeping, and, hopefully, a B in parenting. In my case, I have to give myself a C in organization, and I'm sure Bonnie would give me an A+ in procrastination.

Children have a lot of things they work on simultaneously. As with adults, they'll put greater importance on some things than they will on others. As parents, we need to have the wisdom to be loose and discriminating in assessing our kids. If we try to keep our children performing at an A+ level in all areas of their lives, we deserve a D or F in that part of parenting. In our practice, we sometimes see children who are burned-out at fifteen or sixteen because of the pressure their parents put on them to be exceptional in all areas of their life.

Take a minute to see if you are keeping the big picture of each of your children. Look at their failings from their point of view. A fuller appreciation of your children will keep you more balanced in dealing with them. It wouldn't hurt to apply the same criterion to your spouse, your friends and yourself. Remember the Lord's Prayer: "Forgive us our trespasses as we forgive those who trespass against us." The big picture helps us keep balanced psychologically and spiritually. We decrease our stress level keeping us emotionally stable, and we are more inclined to accept others for who they are, not what they do. This panoramic frame of mind puts us in a better position to nurture the souls of others, especially of our child.

5. TV

Several years ago our family tried an experiment: we shut the TV off completely for a month. Bonnie agreed easily. She doesn't watch it that much. It was my idea so I had to accept it. Our children said okay — after I consented to pay them a small sum each day.

The results were wonderful. We found ourselves talking more to each other. We noticed our children coming into the breakfast nook more often, our usual family meeting place. There was a definite improvement in more intimate interaction between all of us. There were even some surprise benefits like my son saying one time, "Well, I might as well do my homework. I don't have anything else to do."

After the month, we turned on the set again. But the lasting effect has been that TV has never been as important in our family. We are in better balance. TV doesn't control us.

This experience taught me first hand what a disconnector TV can be in spite of its marvelous potential. Even if the whole family is watching the same program, they are in parallel positions, not face-to-face contact. They are all looking straight ahead and not at each other. Conversations are often carried on while watching TV. Children, who have spent so many hours of their formative years glued to the TV set, are not used to looking at others, eyeball to eyeball. In many families children have TV in their bedrooms. They have access to it any hour of the day or night.

We believe children won't be harmed by watching some television. In fact, since popular shows are the subject of conversation among peers, familiarity with them can help children socialize. I recall listening to radio shows like *The Lone Ranger* and *The Green Hornet.* Part of our childhood conversation and play revolved around imitating the characters and reciting the lines from these programs. Children do the same today. We have to be careful not to demonize TV in our efforts to protect our children.

But just like everything else in life, we have to take a balanced approach to TV, especially in regard to our children. To get back in control of your family and become better balanced we make the following suggestions:

No TV during meals. Meals are for sharing not only food but the daily stories of each family member. Mealtime is our opportunity to strengthen our family connections and to comfort one another. It is also a good time to teach children how to talk to adults.

By learning to talk to adults, children increase their ability to express themselves more clearly. If, during dinner, your nine-year-old has the full attention of her parents when she tells them about her teacher, she increases her sense of self-worth. On the contrary, the child whose parents are always glued to the television set during mealtime may begin to doubt that anyone finds him interesting.

Excessive TV diminishes the family's ability to entertain each other. Children develop better verbal skills, they learn more quickly, and they cooperate better when parents are involved with them. When was the last time you played board games, cards or *Pictionary* with your children? Children get to know the fun sides of their parents by games such as *Monopoly.* Unfortunately, TV and VCRs have become the major source of family entertainment. TV has made the interaction between family members more remote and passive. Set aside one night a week for the family to play games together. I guarantee you'll see a big difference in family interaction.

No TV in each child's room. Unfortunately, this has become quite common. In a poll conducted jointly by Nickelodeon cable network and Yankelovich Partners Inc., seventy-five percent of the 1,341 children ages six to seventeen interviewed had their own room. Fifty-nine percent of these had their own television set in their room. We feel children need prudent supervision in their choice of programs. Left by themselves, TV can become the main source of their information about their world. And parents often are not even aware of what their children are learning.

While we are not suggesting you turn TV off for a month, you might consider turning it off for a day occasionally. Your kids will howl like banshees; they'll think you are from the Middle Ages; they'll be embarrassed to tell their friends; they won't understand — at least not until they are parents. What may happen, after the initial shock, is the family will turn to each other as a source of nurturing.

When my children wanted to tell me something or ask me a question while I was watching TV, I found half of me listening to them and the other half tuned to Monday night football. During our no-TV month, I got used to paying full attention to their requests and problems. I liked it. They liked it. Now when I'm watching TV and they come to talk to me, I shut the set off immediately. (Bonnie appreciates it, too, when she wants my attention.) Without the electronic interference, I feel more in control and better balanced. With my full attention on my children, I have a better chance to nurture their souls because I'm more attuned to observing and understanding them. Nurturing the soul accepts no half-hearted efforts, no distracted connections.

Our children's TV time should be limited. In general, the less time they spend in front of the set the better. Many children are now watching it more hours than they spend in school. Watching TV can become hypnotic. We question if TV, sometimes, is a form of self-medication that children (and adults) may use to mask anxiety and depression.

6. Parallel Lives

To keep our psychological and spiritual balance and have reasonable control, we offer the idea of "parallel lives." Phil, my friend from boyhood, was comparing the difference between his life at eighteen and his life now at sixty.

"Then, all I worried about was school, a part-time job, and keeping enough fuel in my gas-guzzling Chevy," he says ruefully. "Now, forty years later, life has become so complicated. I worry about my job, my retirement, my marriage, my kids and grandkids, my health, taking care of my eighty-year-old mother — I could go on and on."

Phil was expressing what many people feel about responsibilities from home, family, work, friends, relatives, church and community. My boyhood friend brought to mind a colleague's response when, meeting him in our mutual office building, I wished him a Happy New Year. "I'm afraid I'll have to wait several years for my year to be happy," he said. He was missing an essential part of keeping balanced: finding time to enjoy life despite one's responsibilities, pressure and problems.

Parallel lives means care for ourselves should not be eliminated by other duties. The life of fun, relaxation, and reflection has to run parallel to our lives as parents, spouses, workers, citizens, church members, and whatever other roles we play in life.

We need to develop the skill of *compartmentalization* — a big word for the simple idea of not letting any one element of our lives overrun the others. Some men seem better at this than women. Perhaps it has something to do with the male working more out of the left side of his brain, the center of logic and analysis. The female works out of both sides of her brain simultaneously. The right side is the center of emotions and relationships. Often it's more problematic for her to put limits on her family obligations. For example, a man has ten jobs to do on Saturday. He finishes five and comfortably postpones (compartmentalizes) the remaining five while he parks himself in front of the tube to watch football. A woman starts out on the same Saturday with ten jobs. But by the time she's finished five, she's discovered an additional fifteen. While she is putting her son's clean clothes in his dresser, she notices his shoes need to be cleaned and that one shoelace is broken. Picking up the shoes, she sees several new spots on the bedroom carpet — "Better get a wet rag right away to see if the *Scotch Guard* works," she thinks. And so on and so on until she collapses at 9:00 p.m. She'd help herself more by learning to compartmentalize her responsibilities. Of course, it might help her if the man in her life compartmentalized less.

The concept of parallel lives is especially difficult for many women. I know Bonnie finds it difficult to relax at home. She doesn't settle back until we're about a mile away. She has difficulty turning off the "call" of laundry, dishes, cleaning, dinner, shopping lists, kids' clothes, and on and on.

To develop parallel lives in our family, Bonnie and I have started what we call our "Fun Calendar." We plan certain activities and enjoy looking forward to them during the year. Last year we purchased tickets for the Los Angeles Civic Opera's *Porgy and Bess.* We ordered them nine months in advance. During this time, we were able to listen to the music, familiarize ourselves with the play, and enjoy it many times before we actually saw it.

Make a priority list of the "lives" you have. In what place is your life of fun, relaxation and reflection? Are you like my colleague, who feels he has to wait for a few years before he can have some happiness? Start a "Fun Calendar." Work at *compartmentalizing* your lives. Having fun is not automatic. You have to *make* it happen.

"Parallel lives" helps us to keep balanced. It gives us a sense of control over our lives. It allows us to slow down, to smell the roses, to set up priorities, and to find joy in our lives. In such an atmosphere, it's easier to nurture the soul.

7. Oliver's Law

My wife and I discovered how marital expectations can catch you by surprise. One evening, very early in our marriage, I came home from work, and Bonnie told me the dining room chandelier was not working. "When can you fix it?" she asked. Dutifully, I changed the light bulbs and turned on the switch. That was the only repair I was able to offer. Of course, the chandelier did not respond. We looked at each other and realized certain basic assumptions would have to change.

Bonnie comes from a family where her father, two brothers and two brothers-in-law seem to be able to tear down and rebuild a complete house in a single day. I grew up in a Chicago flat where only the janitor was allowed to make repairs. My experience with electrical problems was limited to turning on switches and changing light bulbs. Mr. Fix-it I'm not.

Enter Oliver. We found Oliver through a mutual friend from Chicago (another graduate of the flats). Oliver became both our handyman and, along with his wife Gladys, our friends. He also saved us a lot of money we probably would otherwise have spent on marital therapy.

Oliver was in his middle-seventies when we first met him. He was retired but had found a new career in helping homeowners like ourselves. For the ten years he was our handyman (he died a few years ago), we watched him tackle one problem after another. Besides his considerable skills in every area of our home, we were most impressed by his patience in sticking to a job without ever losing his cool. One day Bonnie asked him how he managed to keep so calm when so many unexpected and complicated issues arose while repairing something.

Oliver enjoyed describing the way he saw life. He was part philosopher. That day he was working on a particularly thorny problem with a leaky pipe underneath the kitchen sink. He put his tools down and said, "Every morning I start the day figuring I'll have at least ten problems or ten things happen that I didn't expect. If I only run into four or five I feel I've had a pretty good day. If I run into all ten, well, it's only what I expected. That usually keeps me in a pretty good mood so I don't have any reason to be disappointed. That's how I keep my balance."

Bonnie and I have found this common-sense approach to daily problems so helpful that we often bring him up in our talks. *Oliver's Law* has helped us accept reality and avoid living in a fantasy world. If we believe that problems are the exception and not the rule, we are building castles in the air. Obstacles are as much a part of life as the air we breathe. Once we accept this, we're not thrown off balance when difficulties pop up. I have found that Oliver's attitude has helped me accept my own limitations and to be less judgmental of the problems others have.

Bonnie describes how, when our children were toddlers, she would wake up each morning hoping for a smooth, enjoyable day. When one of the kids had a high fever, earache or similar problem her day could be disrupted running to the doctors, getting the medicine and devoting all her waking and most of her sleeping hours to caring for our children. Oliver helped her to see that "normal" includes unanticipated obstacles. A problem-free day is the exception, not vice-versa as many of us unrealistically think.

8. Words and Respect

The pen is mightier than the sword. Our words reveal what we think and feel about others and ourselves. We use words to communicate joy, sadness, love and hate. Words are powerful. They can warm or freeze the soul. Winston Churchill's words inspired the English to stand firm against Hitler. Martin Luther King's dream that his children would be judged not by the color of their skin but by the content of their character inspired our nation to move toward racial equality. Ghandi's words forced a country to recognize the power of nonviolence.

Respect between children and parents begins with words. Infants, before they have developed the use of language, are affected by their parents' words. "Pumpkin, Sweetie, Darling, My Precious," cooed by a doting parent, are already shaping the infant's self-respect. Just as "Stop crying, you spoiled brat!" screamed by an irritated parent can sow the seeds of self-disgust.

You may think that Bonnie and I drive a Model T Ford or that I wear spats on my shoes when we tell you what we believe should be the tolerance level for all inappropriate words (swearing, cussing, profanities) between parents and children. ZERO! Words teach children the boundaries they need to have to feel secure with their parents and other adults in their life. We have found that children who are not allowed to use inappropriate words to their parents and whose parents follow the same rule have mutual respect. The indiscriminate use of four letter words on TV and in film seems to be a symptom of the loss of respect we see today.

"Respect" lights up the path in the searching for the souls of our children. The word itself comes from the Latin meaning *to look back* or *to regard*. Without showing regard for each other in the very words we use, there is less chance of nurturing each other's souls. Parents who customarily unleash a salvo of four-letter words not only damage their children's ears but also wound their souls.

9. Spanking

We don't recommend spanking. By spanking we mean the deliberate, usually multiple striking with the hand on the bottom of a child. Hitting on the upper part of the body or on the legs with a spoon, belt, paddle, or other instrument is abusive by our standards. We have carefully examined the pros and cons of spanking and have concluded that the cons outweigh the pros by a wide margin. Some believe there are benefits from spanking, at least from the parent's viewpoint. It is a clear, quick method of addressing the problem. Children get the point of your not wanting a certain behavior to continue. Control is established, at least temporarily. However, we believe the emotional cost to the children and parents from spanking is too great.

We believe there are better ways to shape and guide our children, ways which help maintain psychological and spiritual balance in the family.

Spanking may say more about the failure of the parent than the undesirable behavior of the child, just as the growing violence of young people may say more about the failure of society than the crimes of children. I taught high school in Chicago in an era when physical punishment of students by teachers was permitted. It didn't take me long to learn that only the poor teachers had to control their students by this method. The good teachers hardly had to raise their voices to keep order.

From the beginning, we need to shape and guide our children by *moral authority*. This exists in families where parents assume responsibility and take charge of their kids. Children grow up accepting that mom and dad are in charge. Moral authority is based on love and respect, parents toward their children and children toward their parents. It is not despotic, punitive nor authoritarian. Children are not possessions. As children mature in age and experience, parents joyfully give them an ever-increasing responsibility for themselves. When children are ready to challenge this system seriously and believe it no longer works for them, they are ready to move out on their own.

Where parents have moral authority over their children, they have no reason to fear their children growing bigger and stronger. If a father's authority over his sons is based on physical power, dad may not welcome their increasing prowess since it may well be turned against him some day. Such a father can block the natural development of his sons by this unhealthy competition. Dad doesn't pass the baton on to the next generation. On the other hand, when a father knows his moral authority is respected by his children, then he welcomes and celebrates their growth and accomplishments, especially when they surpass him.

Since I married late, I wasn't able to physically interact with my son the same way I would have had I been much younger. When we would play catch, he accepted the fact that he had to retrieve *his* missed catches and *mine* as well. I had made a bet with him that the day he could pin me in a wrestling match, I would give him five dollars. Being athletic and working out with weights, he got very strong by the time he was in his middle teens. Each time we wrestled, I became aware of his increasing physical power. Bonnie began to worry that if I kept trying to compete with him on this level, she was afraid I'd have a heart attack. She suggested I concede the match and give him the five dollars, which I did. It was a sad day for both my son and myself even though we knew it was the prudent thing to do. I passed the baton to him without feeling that my moral authority over him decreased in any way.

Spanking sends a message that the stronger have the right to control the weaker. It runs the risk that children see their parents as bullies. They may not distinguish between the parent's actions and the parent's intention. ("This is for your own good. It hurts me more than it hurts you.")

We believe another negative feature of spanking is that *practice makes perfect.* The more you spank, the easier it becomes. The proponents of this punitive method of discipline advise that it be used cautiously and always when one is calm. However, human nature being what it is, and given the increasing stress that families live under today, it's very tempting to turn quickly and frequently to spanking for a "quick fix." In our experience with families over these many years, we have observed that once parents justify spanking, even for religious reasons, they may revert to it more often and for more minor offenses. We believe that spanking can throw the family off balance psychologically and spiritually.

We are especially opposed to fathers spanking daughters. The burgeoning awareness of domestic violence forces us to reexamine practices which, while solving immediate problems, may be creating more serious ones in the future. We think this may be the case when dad spanks his daughter.

Usually, a daughter's first male contact is with her father. This relationship colors her attitude toward all future, significant men. When a father strikes his daughter, even when he is following the rules laid down by those who are in favor of corporal punishment, this can send a mixed message — that a man can simultaneously love her and physically hurt her. She may be confused when later on she is hit by her husband or boyfriend, who also professes to love her. We believe that fathers who spank put their daughters at risk of not recognizing an abusive relationship when they are adults. Whenever we give talks to parents, we urge fathers not to take that chance for the sake of their daughters' future relationships with men.

A woman whose father never crossed the line of physical punishment learns to expect that a man never lets his anger lead to physical abuse. If she finds herself with a man who is physically abusive, she is more likely to recognize quickly that he is dangerous and is not capable of sustaining a healthy, protective relationship. "My father had lots of reasons to be mad at me," she says, "but he never hit me. This jerk I'm with has a major problem, and I want no part of him." She will thank her dad for demonstrating how a man should respect a woman.

Fathers who hit their sons may be unwittingly contributing to future domestic violence. In almost all cases of domestic violence, the perpetrator, usually a male, has himself been the victim of violence as a child. Our society needs to find ways to stem the rising tide of violence. Each of us has to look into our own lives and recognize what are own attitudes, actions and omissions are contributing to the violence around us. We firmly believe if we had a generation of fathers who dedicated themselves to using their physical strength to protect rather than punish, we would see a significant decrease in domestic violence in the next generation.

10. Storytelling

Susan is twenty-two. She breaks up every time her parents tell the story of her calling the garbage man "gabaga." Matt, her eighteen-year old brother, howls with laughter when his parents describe him at four running down the hallway in his Superman suit convinced he was flying over the city of Metropolis.

Lynn's two children, six-year-old Jennifer and four- year-old Albert, get totally absorbed when their mother goes over their baby pictures telling the stories they've heard dozens of times. Children, at whatever age, love to hear stories about themselves.

One of the most popular couples' retreats Bonnie and I give is based on "Storytelling." Couples reconnect through their shared history: how they met, their wedding, significant moments in their lives together. Like a flashback, memories and feelings come flooding in, washing away the years. The most touching moment of the weekend is when we play a recording of "I Could Write a Book" from "Pal Joey" by Richard Rodgers and Lorenz Hart. The remembered commingling of their shared stories moves both the men and women to tears.

Unfortunately, storytelling has become a lost art in many families. We have become enmeshed in the lives and stories of celebrities. Our children know more about the lives of the stars of TV sitcoms than about their parents and grandparents.

Storytelling links us to ourselves and to the close people in our lives. The story of all of us is in some way the story of each of us. One reason that psychotherapy helps is that it's probably the first time a person has the chance to tell his or her own story to a supportive, nonjudgmental person. In telling our story to another, we learn about ourselves. We catch a glimpse of our souls. A Dutch proverb says, "Shared grief is half grief; shared joy is double joy."

Look at the rapt faces of little children as they listen to a story being read to them. Their souls are touched as they identify with the cast of characters in the story, discovering new parts of themselves.

Stories heal. People who have lost loved ones in a tragedy cannot rest until they hear the full story. Our friends Mary and Jim, who had lost their seventeen-year-old son in a water-skiing accident, needed to hear as much as they could from the people who were with Todd when he died. They went back to the lake where the accident happened; they looked at the boat which was pulling him; they even had to look at the single ski he was using. They explained to me that they needed to find out as much as they could about the last hours of their son's life. They knew that the life-long process of healing such horrendous grief could not even begin until they knew the full story.

When Ann was pregnant for the first time, her mother gave her a wonderful present, a written description of the events surrounding Ann's own birth: how it was for her parents; why they had chosen the name Ann; what they did to prepare Ann's room and crib; and how her father brought flowers for Baby Ann and her mother. It so touched Ann that she is writing the story of her own child's birth, to put it away, and present it when her child is about to become a parent. Stories connect generations to each other.

When your children are young, write down the funny things they do and say. Later on, they will love to hear you retell these times. As they get older, take an occasional trip down memory lane with your photo album, reliving the moments caught in the pictures. Ask your children what stories and incidents they remember. You'll be surprised at their responses. Recently, my twenty-one-year old son recalled how, when he was three, I used to sit him on my knee and sing *Pony Boy*. When I got to the part of "Whoa, my Pony Boy," he remembers that I would open my legs, then catch him, screaming with delight, as he started to fall. Such stories warm the souls of both parents and children.

11. Rituals

Rituals help a child in two ways. 1) They make the world safer and more predictable. 2) They give him/her a clearer sense of self.

When my daughter was two, she had a bedtime ritual of lining up all six of her cuddly, stuffed animals in the identical way each night. Snoopy, her main pal, was next to her. Then came Bunny Rabbit, Teddy Bear, Pooh Bear, Giraffe, and Momma Lion. I remember the line-up well because she was adamant about the order. Whenever I was in a hurry, putting Pooh Bear after Giraffe or Teddy Bear before Bunny Rabbit, she let me know the ritual was broken. As soon as I had properly arranged all her little animal family, she would peacefully slip into slumber. Now her world was safe and secure.

Rituals bring consistency to children. Bedtime rituals like putting on pajamas, taking a bath, brushing teeth, saying prayers, and reading a story are important for making children feel safe and secure. When parents are inconsistent about these nighttime rituals, children can turn a comforting, tender time into a nightmare. We advise parents who are having problems with their children at bedtime to set up a consistent line-up of rituals. First, brush their teeth; second, put on their pajamas; third, say their prayers; and so on — establishing a predictable ritual each night. Nine times out of ten, the parents marvel at how pleasant bedtime becomes. The ritual comforts the child. It nurtures the soul.

Rituals also shed light on who we are. Recently, we attended the funeral of the mother of a Jewish friend of ours. At the burial site, we were impressed by the distinctive Jewish rituals: the Hebrew incantations of the Rabbi, the men and boys wearing the *yarmulke,* and every person in attendance putting a shovelful of dirt on the coffin. These ceremonial symbols were very meaningful to our friend's family. Later, the family shared with us how comforting it was and how connected they felt to Grandma by taking part in the religious service they remembered since childhood. The ritual touched their souls.

Even though Bonnie and I left professional religious life many years ago, we are still deeply touched by solemn Masses where the choir sings Gregorian Chant in Latin. The music and the ritualistic ceremony penetrates our souls, reminding us of our spiritual roots.

Children don't find all valuable rituals pleasant. Bonnie and I decided to raise our children as Catholics since this religious expression has been such a part of our lives. Part of this included going to Mass on Sunday, a boring activity for most young people. I remember my children grabbing my wrist every thirty seconds, hoping it was time to go home. They thought if they stared at the watch often enough and hard enough, they could make the time go faster. We believe the inconvenience children suffer from such rituals as church or visiting relatives is a small price to pay to establish their identity.

Families benefit from their own customs and rituals. We recommend that they establish the custom of eating together — if not every day, at least once a week. If your children know from an early age that eating together is an inviolable ritual, a strong sense of identity develops. Unfortunately today, many families are so scattered by the interference of divorce, blended families, two-career parents, and unpredictable schedules that ties have been weakened. Children may suffer a lack of identity. The alienation of so many of our young people comes from their lack of strong family bonds. Rituals are threads that keep the fabric of the family and society closely interwoven.

Conclusion

Many people spend much time and energy developing their minds and their bodies, but neglecting their souls. This psychological and spiritual imbalance has affected our children as well. "The parents have eaten sour grapes and the children's teeth are set on edge." (Ezekiel 18:2) In our efforts to get our children ready for a competitive, achievement-oriented world, we are neglecting to nurture their souls.

However, the good news is that today parents are waking up, aware that something valuable is missing. They are recognizing that no amount of money, achievement, status, or recognition seems to satisfy their need for something deeper.

Today there is an immense groundswell among parents of all racial, ethnic, political or religious persuasions. "Spirituality" and "soul" are being talked about openly. People are hungry for more than the constant bombardment of consumer-driven items offered in the menu of commercial advertising. Parents want to connect with their children in a more profound way. They want to offer them values that will not only help them be successful materially but also fulfilled spiritually; not only productive in their careers but also contributing to their community; not only involved in self-fulfillment but also committed to their families.

In a real sense, we are engaged in a struggle to free the souls of our children. Because they are vulnerable, impressionable and malleable, children need to be protected. This is best done by parents nurturing their souls. We hope these pages will help you as parents to do just that.